to $\mathcal{G}$

ABOUT THE COVER: The crown of thorns is the symbol of Yeshua, King of the Jews, who earned His right to reign over the hearts of His people and the world by His obedience to His Father unto death. The Star of David is the symbol of Yeshua's Davidic birthrite to the throne of Israel. The powerful, dynamic appearance of this symbol, conceived by Phil Goble and designed by Bob Lovett, is meant to suggest the world-astounding growth of Messianic Judaism in these end times (Romans 11:26).

Everything You Need to Grow a Messianic Synagogue

Phillip E. Goble

William Carey Library

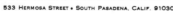

533 HERMOSA STREET • SOUTH PASADENA, CALIF. 91030

For more copies and bulk order discount, contact the publisher.

Library of Congress Cataloging in Publication Data

Goble, Phillip E   1943-
    Everything you need to grow a Messianic synagogue.

    1. Jewish Christians.   2. Missions to Jews.
I.   Title.
BR158.G6   248'.246   74-28017
ISBN 0-87808-421-5

In accord with some of the most recent thinking in the academic press, the William Carey Library is pleased to present this scholarly book which has been prepared from an author-edited and author-prepared camera-ready manuscript.

Published by the William Carey Library
533 Hermosa Street
South Pasadena, Calif. 91030
Telephone 213-799-4559

PRINTED IN THE UNITED STATES OF AMERICA

This book is dedicated
to my wife Janice,
who edited and typeset
the entire manuscript,
and to my Jewish brothers everywhere.

Contents

*These page numbers refer to those at the bottom.

Foreword

The Reverend Phillip Goble is an associate minister of one of the fastest growing Messianic Synagogues in the world today, Beth Emanuel in Encino, California. Reverend Goble and I have worked together for three years developing an effective discipling method for people of Jewish origin.

I met Reverend Goble while he was a student at Fuller Theological Seminary where he was working on his doctorate. I was immediately impressed with the straightforwardness of his approach and his methodical thinking. Sensing Reverend Goble would have much to offer an up-and-coming Jewish outreach ministry, I asked him to come on the Beth Emanuel Fellowship staff where he has labored most effectively among Jewish people these past several years. His personal dedication to Jewish evangelism and his concern for winning the "lost sheep of the House of Israel" are second to none. I have immeasurably appreciated his faithfulness to the task at hand.

Out of his deep love and concern for Jewish people, Reverend Goble has compiled for his readers the step by step discipling method we have used at Beth Emanuel for some time now. This method — the interlocking document discipling approach — has proven its effectiveness repeatedly. It works and works well in taking Jewish people in their present spiritual condition all the way to genuine Messianic discipleship.

While there is only one avenue to God, only one road to salvation, and only one Saviour, the discipling of Jewish people can be done in two different ways.

The normal way is to innocently but gradually "gentilize" the Jewish believer by naively teaching him to equate many non-Jewish cultural characteristics with the "Gospel Truth" and real "holy" living.

The other, and far better way by all current mission

strategy and thought, is to win Jewish people to the Lord Jesus without nonchalantly or unintentionally divorcing them from their Jewish cultural heritage. We prefer to encourage Jewish believers to maintain Jewish community ties and to enjoy their Jewishness to the maximum. Jesus can be the Lord of one's Jewishness too!

The normal discipling method which unintentionally removes the Jewish believer from his community undermines his effectiveness in winning other Jewish people to the Lord. The unbelievers feel he has abandoned his people, not willing to bear the "reproach" of being Jewish in a "Christian" country.

The Jewishness approach, so suspiciously viewed by many Christians, is where our hope is in seeing tens of thousands of Jewish people saved. More than ever before, the Jewish believer identifies with his people. Everything he does, he has a Jewish reason for doing.

This book, which is for the purpose of helping believers everywhere establish effective ministries among the Chosen People, has such a method in view. The real purpose for Jewish evangelism is not to make Jewish people culturally gentile but to indeed help them become better Jews by personally receiving as Saviour and Lord the Jewish Messiah Jesus!

October, 1974   Reverend Ray Gannon
                                                  Encino, California

Preface

Choosing the wrong cultural specialist as their mentor, Jewish evangelists have typically tried to mimic the apostle to the Gentiles (Paul) and have largely ignored his highly successful (Acts 21:20) cultural counterpart, the apostle to the Jews (James). James was concerned that no "irksome restrictions" (Acts 15:19) be imposed on Gentiles. He would have also been concerned to have no "irksome restrictions" placed on him and the Jerusalem Messianic Synagogue of which he was the pastor. Can you imagine James' reaction if some Gentiles had told his congregation they could no longer practice circumcision or keep kosher? (see Acts 21:20-21). Unfortunately, the dismal history of Jewish missions has been the largely futile effort to impose the irksome restrictions of Gentile culture on Jews. Instead of helping plant and pastor New Testament-patterned Messianic Synagogues with cultural integrity in Jewish neighborhoods like James did in Jerusalem, Jewish ministers typically function as unwitting twentieth century "Gentilizers," trying to persuade Jews to assimilate into Gentile churches — a cultural betrayal the Jewish community understandably resists as ethnic suicide. The Church in a Jewish neighborhood must not forget where she is (I Corinthians 9:20-21), nor should she confuse spiritual and cultural conversion.

When the Church finds herself in a Jewish community she must not shrink from wearing once again her full Jewish dress, all her old synagogue attire. For local churches in Jewish communities to remain inflexibly groomed for Gentiles and then demand that Jews convert to Gentile ways of life and worship in order for Jewish people to accept their own Messiah is the damnable ancient Judaizing heresy in reverse, and must not be tolerated.

✓ The truth is, every church must be culturally relevant to and negotiable with the community it serves or it will serve neither God nor its community. What the Jewish community needs to be saved are thousands of growing synagogues with home Torah studies, yahmakahs, Jewish music, Jewish food, Yiddish jokes, Jewish humor, Jewish customs, ceremonies, holidays, traditions, testimonies, special events, and everything revolving around and pointing toward a very Jewish Yeshua who is Lord of all, Jews and Gentiles as well. Such synagogues can throw their doors open wide with the confidence that God will fill them with Jewish souls and also with people who are of non-Jewish descent but are nevertheless true, born-again, spiritual Jews. These truly born-again believers in Yeshua, unlike many anti-semitic nominal "Christians," love the Jews in all their Jewishness.

What has been needed for a long time is a comprehensive evangelistic tool designed to further the planting and growth of Messianic Synagogues. That is why this book was written. The approach it uses is called the interlocking document method of incorporational evangelism.

The only Evangelist is, of course, God's Holy Spirit. He uses many instruments, many tools. He has used this tool and blessed it greatly to the increase of his households. It is offered to Messianic Jews and other disciples of Yeshua Ha Mashiach with a prayer that they may find it useful in carrying his message to the ends of the earth. Let it be said here, and assumed from this point forward: nothing in this book has any value unless it is bathed in prayer, anointed by the Holy Spirit, and accomplished through servants who are sensitive to the leading of God. Let it also be understood here that the term "spiritual Jew" as it is Scripturally defined in this book, includes only those who have submitted in faith to Yeshua as Lord through the rite of Spiritual circumcision, the mikveh-bris of water immersion.

This book is a series of detachable, interlocking documents which lead the Jewish inquirer into progressively deeper levels of commitment until he has become a member of a Messianic Synagogue of Yeshua. Besides much culturally relevant material for pre-baptismal (Part II) and pre-membership counseling (Part III), the book also contains a very Jewish celebration of Holy Communion and a Messianic Friday Evening Service (Part IV), as well as an appendix on starting Jewish home Bible studies and turning them quickly into

Messianic Synagogue congregations. The book is intended to be complete enough that a young man in a Jewish neighborhood can order 50 copies and in two years be the pastor of a growing 50-member Messianic Synagogue congregation.

The book was developed in Los Angeles through the cooperation of Ray Gannon, who is the spiritual leader of the fastest growing Messianic Synagogue in the United States. Beth Emanuel congregation is made up chiefly of Jews and a few Gentiles and has seen 70 Jewish people baptized in less than 18 months, going from a small home Bible study to a $187,000 Messianic Synagogue in 2½ years.

Let me explain how this book might help you. Suppose you were an evangelist trying to reach the Jewish people in your city. Suppose you started a Bible study in a Jewish home, and then ordered 50 copies of this book.

Since *Everything You Need to Grow a Messianic Synagogue* is a 4-part book, each part is an interlocking document designed to lead people step by step toward Part IV, which is the Messianic Synagogue Member's Manual. Each part is torn out of its binding and given to the person separately, so that in order to be given Part III, the person must first respond affirmatively to Part II, which means agreeing to be baptized. Likewise, in order to read Part IV, he must first respond affirmatively to Part III, which means getting baptized and signing the Messianic Synagogue membership application. Each time a part is given to a person and he responds affirmatively, he returns that part and it goes back into its respective binder. Then he is given the next part until he is prepared to receive Part IV, in which case he receives the binder itself with the entire book in it as well as the right hand of fellowship to become an incorporated Messianic Synagogue member.

Therefore, a new believer is discipled by the interlocking documents in the following way. He reads Part I and becomes oriented and more interested. He reads Part II and prays to receive Yeshua and agrees to come to the Messianic Synagogue to take the mikveh on Acts 2:42 Sunday, the last Sunday of every month. On that day, just before he is baptized, the person who is going to baptize him reads him Part IIIA, baptizes him, and gives him the entire document, including IIIB, which is the membership application. If the application is returned in time, he can be received as a member and be given his synagogue membership binder with all 4 parts in it

by the next Acts 2:42 Sunday. Then he will be able to re-read
Parts I, II, and III and to read for the first time Part IV, which
is the synagogue member's manual.

Now let's say you pray that God will give you a name for
your Messianic Synagogue and God gives you the name "Beth
Israel." So you order 50 inexpensive, yet attractive 5½ x 8½
3-ring vinyl binders with the words "Beth Israel" on the front
in gold letters. You put your fifty copies of this book into
your 50 binders, coding each binder with a number, 1-50,
and putting each binder's number on Part I, Part II, and
Part III of its respective contents. Then, keeping record of
each person's name and binder number, you "check out"
Part I to the people of your home Torah study. When you ask
each person to read it so they can return it to be given Part II,
the number you fixed on Part I will help you return it to its
proper binder. Thus as people move from Part I to Part II to
Part III, they return each part; and, as they respond to it in
obedience, they receive the next part. All this time the
binder's number on its various parts keeps the binder complete and in order.

In this way it is much better not to give the entire book to
an unsaved Jewish person at one time, but rather to lay aside
a binder for that person and give him only one part at a time,
at the rate he or she can digest it as the Holy Spirit moves that
individual toward readiness for the next phase of commitment
involved in each succeeding part. By assigning a binder number
for each person, you keep track of which individuals have
which parts (that's the purpose of the binder's number on its
parts) and follow them up. These pages are too valuable to be
collecting dust in someone's attic. If a person gets endlessly
frozen at any level short of Part IV, he should return the part
so that what would have become his binder will again be complete and can be used to disciple someone else.

Because of the special nature of this book, I wish to
acknowledge my debts here rather than elsewhere. The
concise, accurate translation of the New English Bible was
a helpful reference in the composition of my renderings of
the text. Acknowledgment is made for those portions directly
quoted from that copyrighted work. For the theological in-
sights I gleaned from the lectures of my Fuller Theological
Seminary professors, I thank Dr. George Ladd, Dr. James
Daane, Dr. Ralph Martin, Dr. Paul Jewett, and Dr. Daniel
Fuller. Echoes of their wisdom undergirded my own thinking

in this book, and provided a sound Scriptural guide for the Jewish theology I have produced. My thanks to Bill Anderson, Margie Meese, Margie and Van Moore for their contributions to the production of the final manuscript, as well as Bob Lovett for his illustrations. I also acknowledge my debt to the missiological thinking of Donald McGavran and the faculty of the Fuller School of World Missions, especially Peter Wagner, without whose interest this book might never have seen publication. Finally, I thank all the people of Beth Emanuel Synagogue and especially Ray Gannon for his many helpful suggestions and ideas.

It is the hope of the author of this book that hundreds of growing Messianic Synagogues will be established in the United States and the rest of the world. There is no way the 6 million Jewish people in America can be effectively reached without hundreds of growing Messianic Synagogues like the one Ray Gannon and I planted in Los Angeles. It is our prayer that God will give you the same privilege he gave us and reward your evangelistic toil with the fruit of a New Testament-patterned Messianic Synagogue. Baruch ha shem!

October, 1974   Phil Goble

Part One

What Is Messianic Judaism?

Contents

WHAT IS MESSIANIC JUDAISM?

*These page numbers refer to those at the top.

I
What Is Messianic Judaism?

Many people, including some followers of Yeshua (Jesus' Hebrew name), like to see a sharp distinction between Judaism and Christianity. However, the distinction is not so clear. In fact, if by "Judaism" we mean the true Messianic, Biblical religion of Israel, then the religion that is usually called "Christianity" could really be labeled "Judaism." In reality "Christianity" is true, culturally all-inclusive Messianic Judaism.

JUDAISM FOR THE NATIONS

Messianic Judaism, when it accommodates itself culturally to Gentiles, is properly called "Christianity." However, Messianic Judaism needs no other name when it orients itself ethnically to the very people from whom it originated, the Jews.

It was from the Jews that the world received Messianic Judaism and the Jewish Messiah Yeshua. Even the New Testament, which is the Jewish New Covenant Holy Scriptures, was written by Jews.

It was also from the Jews that we received the world-wide Messianic Synagogue of Yeshua, at first composed exclusively of physical Jews and now comprising spiritual Jews from every race on earth. Unfortunately, many people are ignorant of the fact that the universal Church is nothing other than a culturally all-adaptable Messianic Synagogue. This Messianic Synagogue, though it is capable of changing into every manner of ethnic attire, from a teepee Bible study to an igloo prayer meeting, nevertheless always wears its basic synagogue apparel, ✓ the Jewish Scriptures and the Jewish rituals. Its Jewish rituals are the mikveh bath, which is the standard Jewish

3

means of making proselytes to Judaism, and the Lord's Supper, which is the Passover covenant meal of all spiritual Jews who are adherents to Messianic Judaism. It is little wonder the One God of Israel has been able to use a Messianic Synagogue of such cultural adaptability to make spiritual Jews in every people and to spread Messianic Judaism throughout all the nations.

JUDAISM WITH BIBLICAL MONOTHEISM

But does Messianic Judaism actually teach monotheism, that the Lord our God is one Lord? Of course! How could it be Judaism if it didn't?

However, the Jewish Scriptures themselves teach that God has a complexity in his unity such that Man must be created male-and-female-multiplying in order to adequately reflect the image of God (see Genesis 1:27-28). God did not picture himself by creating a solitary man. The threefold picture of two human beings conceiving a third was necessary to reflect the complex unity of the One God of Israel.

The Hebrew word signifying God's complex unity is *echad*, not the word *yachid*. *Yachid* conveys the idea of simple, absolute unity. The Torah does not say, "Shema, Israel, Adonai, Elohenu, Adonai, *Yachid.*" The Torah says the Lord is *echad*, a complex unity.

In Genesis 2:24, God says that when a man marries a woman the two become *echad*, one. This is not an absolute unity, which would make the two simply, absolutely one human being! Rather, a marriage is *echad* because it is a complex unity of two joined into one. On the other hand, in Judges 11:34, Jephthah's only daughter is simply, absolutely one human being so the Bible refers to her as *yachid*. If God's unity were that simple it would not be possible for King David to say, "The Lord said to my Lord" in Psalms 110.

The truth is, God has always had a complexity in his unity, because God has always had his Holy Spirit and his powerful, creative, divine Word. In somewhat the same way that a traffic policeman can have a left hand and a right hand and still be only one traffic policeman, not three, God can have his Holy Spirit and his divine Word and still be only one God, not three Gods.

The One God of Israel sent his divine Word among us as a Man in order to make an eternal kaporrah (blood covering)

4

for our sin so that we might receive the eternal life of God's Holy Spirit. This was God's gift of love to us, so that he could with mercy and justice forgive us and bring us into a new order of life.

However, God's gracious provision through his divine Word Yeshua has forced the whole world into a crisis of decision. When we look into the Jewish face of Yeshua, we are confronted eyeball to eyeball by the divine Word of God himself. We cannot obey the God of Israel nor can we receive his Holy Spirit unless we obey God's Word become Man, Yeshua Ha Mashiach.

Therefore, the task of Messianic Judaism is to lead people to follow the Jewish Messiah Yeshua in order that they may receive the Holy Spirit. Those who really do follow Yeshua, and are not hypocrites as some of his so-called followers have been, become true spiritual Jews and love our Jewish people just as they love our Jewish Messiah.

JUDAISM TRUE TO THE TENACH

The theology of Messianic Judaism preserves the essentials of the faith of Israel that other brands of Judaism have largely lost. For example, Messianic Judaism maintains in the death of Yeshua the Torah's demand for blood sacrifice: "It is the blood that maketh an atonement for the soul" (Leviticus 17:11). Messianic Judaism also preserves the true significance of such Jewish institutions as the high priesthood, the sage, and the prophet, and such Jewish doctrines as those concerning the Messianic king, the Holy Spirit, and salvation. Through the resurrection from the dead of the great high priest, sage, prophet, and Messianic King Yeshua and through the coming of the Holy Spirit at Pentecost A.D. 30, all these Jewish essentials are imperishably maintained.

Messianic Judaism wishes to proclaim "nothing other than what was foretold by the prophets and by Moses: that the Messiah must suffer, and that as the first to rise from the dead, he would announce the dawn to Israel and to the Gentiles" (Acts 26:22-23). *(NEB)*

Where does it say in the Tenach (the Jewish Scriptures) that the Messiah must suffer? Read Isaiah chapter 53 where the Word of God says that "All we like sheep have gone astray . . . and the Lord hath laid on him the iniquity of us all" (Isaiah 53:6). Read also Daniel 9:26 where the Jewish

Scriptures teach "mashiach yicarate" — "The Messiah shall be cut off" — and the Word of God continues, "But not for himself, and the people of the prince that shall come shall destroy the city and the sanctuary." This prophecy was actually fulfilled, just as Yeshua himself predicted (Luke 21:20-24), when the Roman general Titus destroyed the Temple and with it the priesthood and the city of Jerusalem in A.D. 70, 40 years after the death and resurrection of the Jewish Messiah Yeshua.

Where does it say in the Tenach that the dead would resurrect unto new life or that the Messiah would escape the worms of the grave? Read Job 19:25-26 which expresses the hope of Israel, "For I know that my Redeemer liveth, and that he shall stand upon the earth at last, and after my skin has been destroyed, then from my flesh I shall see my God." King David also expressed the hope of Israel, "Therefore my heart is glad and my spirit rejoices: my flesh also shall rest in hope. For thou wilt not leave my soul in hell; neither will thou permit thy Holy One to see corruption" (Psalms 16:9-10).

THE GOOD NEWS OF MESSIANIC JUDAISM

The Good News of Messianic Judaism is that the hope of Israel has been fulfilled! The resurrection has already begun! The first man has already come out of the tomb! And the God of Israel, praised be he, has accomplished it!

We needed a kaporrah to heal our sin guilt before God. God accomplished it! He sent his Messiah to suffer, and "by his stripes we are healed" (Isaiah 53:5).

God accomplished more. We are powerless in ourselves to live as we should. "The human will is deceitful above all things and desperately wicked, who can know it?" (Jeremiah 17:9). We need to turn from trusting in ourselves and receive the Holy Spirit in order to have the power to live as we should both now and hereafter. God accomplished what he promised in the Jewish Scriptures: "I will put my Spirit into you and make you conform to my commandments, and keep my laws and live by them" (Ezekiel 36:27).

However, our sins have separated us and our Holy God (Isaiah 59:2), and our lives are not acceptable to the Lord unless we are indwelt by the Holy Spirit. Therefore, the Jewish prophet Daniel wrote in the Tenach that "Many of them that sleep in the dust of the earth shall awake, some to everlasting life, and some to shame and everlasting contempt" (Daniel 12:1). King David, realizing the need for his own spiritual inner transformation, said, "Create in me a clean heart, O God; and renew a right spirit within me. Cast me not away from thy presence; and take not thy Holy Spirit from me. Restore unto me the joy of thy salvation; and uphold me with thy free spirit" (Psalms 51:10-12).

The Holy Spirit is given only in obedience to the Messiah Yeshua, who will judge all those who reject him. Read Isaiah 42:1: "Behold my Servant, whom I uphold; my chosen one, in whom my soul delights; I have put my Spirit upon him: he shall bring forth judgment to the nations." Isaiah saw that God would one day make an eternal covenant through the Messiah with Israel (Isaiah 55:3), and Jeremiah foresaw that in that day God would make a new covenant with his people. This covenant would involve an inner transformation of humanity, for Jeremiah foresaw that the divine Word would internalize human hearts with the will of God. Then men would know God so intimately they would actually share his will (Jeremiah 31:31-34). Of this New Covenant, Ezekiel predicted that the Holy Spirit in men would make them want to obey God's Word (Ezekiel 36:27). And the Jewish prophet Joel saw that in that day the transforming power of the Holy Spirit would be poured out as never before (Joel 2:28-29), so great would be the number who would be spiritually transformed or born again.

However, most people expected the resurrection to begin and the Holy Spirit to be poured out at the end of the world. Few believed that these mighty acts could occur until the close of human history. What a surprise it was, then, when 120 orthodox Jews stood up in Jerusalem on Pentecost (Shovuos) A.D. 30, and declared that they personally had already seen the first man alive from the grave, that he was the Messiah, the child called *"el gabor"* (mighty God) in Isaiah 9:6, and that he had poured out the eternal Spirit of God on them already, even though human history was still in progress. These Jewish apostles declared that the Messiah was coming again at the end of history to rule the world, but that he had to come the first time to suffer for sins. The Messiah's death was in order that the Father could righteously forgive all sins, since through the death of the Son, no sins had gone unpunished. The God of Israel loved men so much

7

he sent his divine Word among us as a man to "take the rap" for our sins and to rise from the dead in order that he might live in us. Only in this way could Yeshua, the living Torah of God, write himself into our wills forever with a new obedient spirit, the eternal Spirit of God who gives us eternal life. Only in this way could the New Covenant of Judaism be fulfilled, as Jeremiah foretold:

> "Behold, the days are coming, says the Lord, when I will make a new covenant with the house of Israel and the house of Judah, not like the covenant which I made with their fathers when I took them by the hand to bring them out of the land of Egypt, my covenant which they broke, though I was patient with them, says the Lord. But this is the covenant which I will make with the house of Israel after those days, says the Lord: I will put my torah (law) within them, and I will write it upon their hearts; and I will be their God and they shall be my people. And no longer shall each man teach his neighbor and each his brother, saying, 'Know the Lord,' for they shall all know me, from the least of them to the greatest, says the Lord; for I will forgive their iniquity, and I will remember their sin no more" (Jeremiah 31:31-34).

Therefore, the Good News of Messianic Judaism is that the resurrection has already begun through Yeshua, who has already begun to pour out the Holy Spirit on his followers. Consequently, every person may receive the Holy Spirit and be assured of his own personal coming resurrection by obeying Yeshua as Lord and King. What better news could there be?

THE ONLY ISSUE IN JUDAISM

Were these 120 orthodox Jews lying? Had they really seen Yeshua alive or were they making it up? What about the 500 orthodox Jews who claimed to have seen Yeshua at one time (I Corinthians 15:6) — were they lying? Were Rabbi Saul, Peter, James, John and the rest all lying? Most of these Jews died violent deaths, either at the hands of their own people or in the Roman coliseum. When so many eye witnesses were willing to die to verify their testimony regarding the resurrection of Yeshua, who would presume to call them all liars?

Moreover, their testimony was not about a revived corpse. They testified that they had seen the eternal life of God himself, bodily visible to them as eye witnesses (see I John 1:1-4). Yeshua appeared to them in a tangible yet supernatural, spiritual body capable of appearing anywhere, even through locked doors (John 20:26). They were assured that the Father would one day give them an eternal body like the Son's and that they had already received the Holy Spirit as an actual down-payment on their eternal inheritance.

Although they had been frightened and greatly disillusioned when the Messiah was killed, their hope was revived when Yeshua appeared to them not merely once, but ten times during a period of 40 days. With such magnificent assurance undergirding their witness, it is no wonder that 3,000 Jews responded to their message the very first day they preached it (Acts 2:41).

On that day, Sunday morning, Shovuos, A.D. 30, the proclamation went forth that if Jews were to remain committed to Judaism, they must personally commit themselves to the Messiah of Judaism. Since the key ritual for making proselytes to Judaism had been a mikveh bath, the risen Lord Yeshua commanded his followers to go into all the world making proselytes to Messianic Judaism by means of a mikveh bath in the name of the God of Israel. Everyone who responded in faith to the Jewish Messiah would receive the Holy Spirit and become a spiritual Jew and a true adherent of Biblical Judaism. Everyone who refused to believe would be lost, for where there is sin without repentance there is punishment without forgiveness, and where there is no true apostolic teaching, there is no true Judaism.

Therefore, the crucial issue between Messianic Judaism and any other sort of Judaism centers on the hope of the resurrection from the dead. The only question is whether there is such a hope and whether that hope has been realized in the historical resurrection of Yeshua Ha Mashiach. There is no other issue.

A SYNAGOGUE FREE TO BE A SYNAGOGUE

Since the question of the resurrection of Yeshua Ha Mashiach is the only real issue in Judaism, then a Messianic Synagogue is free to be in all ways a Jewish Synagogue, with these conditions:

1)　So long as its doors are open to all (James 2:2-4);
2)　So long as its all-pervading message is the Good News proclamation of the resurrection begun through Yeshua, the risen Lord and appointed Judge (I Corinthians 2:2);

9

3) So long as its teaching is grounded in the Holy Jewish Scriptures from Genesis to Revelation, no more, no less (Revelation 22:18-19);

4) So long as it uses only the mikveh bath and the Passover covenant meal of the Lord's Supper to make proselytes to Messianic Judaism and does not impose circumcision on Gentiles (I Corinthians 7:18; Acts 15:5-11), since there is no salvation in becoming a physical Jew but only in becoming a spiritual Jew through the circumcision of the Holy Spirit (Colossians 2:11-13).

Now, if these scriptural conditions are kept, a Messianic Synagogue is free to be what it is . . . a Jewish synagogue. The Jewish families of such a synagogue circumcise their babies (Leviticus 12:3). When their children become believers in Yeshua and take the mikveh, the Jewish young men and women can witness to their faith in Messianic Judaism through the bar or bat mitzvah confirmation service.

Anyone who quotes scripture such as Galatians 4:8-10, Colossians 2:16-17, or Romans 14:5-6 to prove that the Jewish festivals or holy days are forbidden to Jewish believers in Yeshua is reading the Bible entirely out of context. Paul is not addressing Jewish believers who are celebrating these days in the name of Yeshua; therefore, his words cannot be taken as criticism of believers who are celebrating these days in the name of Yeshua. The Jewish festivals foreshadow the Messiah and are fulfilled in him. However, a shadow cannot highlight anyone, even the Messiah, if it is totally removed from the picture. The Jewish festivals are not obsolete but are good contemporary teachers that point us toward the Jewish New Covenant of Yeshua Ha Mashiach.

Every Jewish ceremony will be acknowledged and pleasing in God's sight if done in the name of the One in whom all Jewish ceremonies are fulfilled. The Scripture teaches that these are matters on which everyone should reach conviction in his own mind (Romans 14:5). Jewish believers in Yeshua can also remain kosher, if they desire (see Acts 21:20 and Romans 14:3). The Scriptural principles here are "whatever you are doing, whether you speak or act, do everything in the name of the Lord Yeshua, giving thanks to God the Father through him" (Colossians 3:17), and "to the Jew I became like a Jew to win Jews" (I Corinthians 9:20).

Of course, only the Bible is authoritative for the faith and practice of a Messianic Synagogue, and the Talmud can never be placed on a par with the Holy Jewish Scriptures, Genesis through Revelation. However, where the Talmud agrees with the Bible, the Talmud may serve as an occasionally useful illustrative teaching of Biblical truth, though its assertions must always stand the test of God's Word, which is true of any non-Biblical book.

✓ When the Church finds herself in a Jewish community she must not shrink from wearing once again her full Jewish dress, all her old synagogue attire. For local churches in Jewish communities to remain inflexibly groomed for Gentiles and then demand that Jews convert to Gentile ways of life and worship in order for Jewish people to accept their own Messiah is the damnable ancient Judaizing heresy in reverse, and must not be tolerated (see Acts 15:1, 19).

✓ The truth is, every church must be culturally relevant to and negotiable with the community it serves or it will serve neither God nor its community. What the Jewish community needs to be saved are thousands of growing synagogues with home Torah studies, yahmakahs, Jewish music, Jewish food, Yiddish jokes, Jewish humor, Jewish customs, ceremonies, holidays, traditions, testimonies, special events, and everything revolving around and pointing toward a very Jewish Yeshua who is Lord of all, Jews and Gentiles as well. Such synagogues can throw their doors open wide with the confidence that God will fill them with Jewish souls and also with people who are of non-Jewish descent but are nevertheless true, born-again, spiritual Jews. These truly born-again believers in Yeshua, unlike many anti-semitic nominal "Christians," love the Jews in all their Jewishness.

Synagogues such as these will give the world-wide Body of Yeshua an enriching, fresh look at her origins. For the leaders of these Messianic Synagogues will not be able to content themselves with blindly imitating reformed, orthodox, and conservative congregations down the street, but will have to continually re-examine the Scriptures to steer Messianic Judaism on its own distinctive course in the world-wide Body of the Messiah's people.

NOTE: *Please return this valuable document. Then the vitally important additional information of Part Two will be made available to you.*

Part Two

The Mikveh-Bris:
Your Glad Response
to the Good News of Messianic Judaism

Contents

THE MIKVEH-BRIS: YOUR GLAD RESPONSE TO THE GOOD NEWS OF MESSIANIC JUDAISM

*These page numbers refer to those at the top.

14

II

The Mikveh-Bris: Your Glad Response to the Good News of Messianic Judaism

Many people do not know that Judaism used to be a missionary religion, and that the official leaders of Judaism were both zealous and highly successful at making converts. In fact, so numerous were the proselytes in Biblical times that there is even a term in Scripture for conversion to Judaism — *mityahadim* (see Esther 8:17).

THE OUTGOING NATURE OF TRUE JUDAISM

The rabbis knew that Judaism was not merely a narrow, national religion. The Talmud says that the teachings of Judaism "were freely meant for all mankind" (Shab. 738), and that God waits "for the nations of the world in the hope that they will turn and be brought under his wings" (Naso X.1). In fact, according to ancient tradition, the first proselytes to the Jewish faith were Abraham and Sarah, and through their descendants God intended to proselytize the nations (see also Matthew 28:19).

Of course, Rabbinic Judaism is no longer a missionary religion. Since the coming of Yeshua, the rabbis have cooled off in their zeal to win converts. However, Messianic Judaism has always been a missionary religion, eager to share the blessings of Judaism with the whole world. In our own era, millions of adherents to Messianic Judaism, including both Jews and Gentiles from every culture and country, have become born-again spiritual Jews and genuine converts to Biblical Judaism. For true commitment to Judaism can only be through true commitment to the Messiah of Judaism, Yeshua Ha Mashiach.

Unfortunately, not all Jews nor all Gentiles have been willing to become proselytes to Messianic Judaism because not

15

everyone is willing to commit himself to the Messiah Yeshua. And many who have committed themselves to the Messiah Yeshua are even ignorant of the fact that what they call "Christianity" is really Messianic Judaism adapted to Gentile culture. Nevertheless, "Christianity" is still true Biblical, Messianic Judaism, whether every believer in Yeshua realizes it or not.

JUDAISM'S INDISPENSIBLE MIKVEH

Scripturally, a Jew is anyone who has renounced idolatry and thrown in his lot with the people of the one true God. Therefore, when a Gentile lady named Ruth clung to Naomi and her God, Ruth became a Jewess, even qualifying to become the great-grandmother of King David.

However, historically, there have been three rites involved in the reception of proselytes into Judaism: 1) circumcision (the bris), 2) water immersion (the mikveh), and 3) a sacrifice (the kaporrah). Rabbi Judah the Patriarch compares this three-fold admission into Judaism as reminiscent of the Biblical history of Israel, a nation circumcised before leaving Egypt (Joshua 5:2), baptized in the desert in a holy washing ritual (Exodus 19:10), and sprinkled with the blood of a covenant sacrifice (Exodus 24:3-8) [see Sifra, Ahare Perek 12].

Nevertheless, the central ritual of admittance into Judaism has always been a mikveh of water immersion. The sacrifice offered by the adherent to Judaism was never as important as circumcision or baptism, especially after the Temple was destroyed, making sacrifice impossible. Furthermore, since women converts to Judaism far outnumbered men, circumcision could hardly become the chief rite of entry into Judaism. Therefore, the **one** indispensible thing that any convert, whether male or female, had to do to become a Jew was to get baptized. Of course, a male had to be circumcised as well, but if we look for the **one** thing that **every** non-Jew — regardless of sex — had to do in order to become a Jew, the answer is: he or she had to submit to a mikveh.

Proselytes crossed the threshold into Israel through an immersion bath, because Israel had entered the promised land through water (the Red Sea) and therefore so must all who would become Jews. There was a definite concept of cleansing built into this decisive mikveh. A heathen who left behind the idolatry of the Gentile world to become a Jew had passed from sin to a whole new life. When he came up out of the water, he was considered ritually undefiled, beginning life all over with a clean bill of goods, like a child newly born. He had begun a new life as a *ben berit,* a son of the covenant, a Jew.

Towards the end of the first century, A.D. the leading rabbis of the school of Hillel claimed that a man was Jewish as soon as he was baptized, the mikveh being as decisive a rite in the case of determining whether a man had become a Jew as it was for making the same determination for a woman (Mishnah Aboth I.12).

Later, in Messianic Judaism, circumcision was not imposed on Gentiles (I Corinthians 7:18; Acts 15:5-11), since there is no salvation in becoming a physical Jew but only in becoming a spiritual Jew through the circumcision of the Holy Spirit. ✓ Therefore, water immersion became the indispensible ritual for all who would become adherents of Messianic Judaism.

THE IMMERSION PRACTICED BY THE JEWISH PROPHET YOCHANAN HA MAHTBEEL

Rabbi Akiba said: "Blessed are you, O Israel. Before whom are you made clean and who makes you clean? Your Father in heaven. As it is written, 'And I will dash clean water upon you and you shall be clean' (Ezekiel 36:25). And again it says, 'O Lord, the *mikveh* (meaning either the word 'hope' or the word 'font') of Israel (Jeremiah 17:13); as the *mikveh* cleanses the unclean, so does the Holy One cleanse Israel' " (Mishnah Yoma 8.9).

The Jewish prophet Ezekiel speaks of God's cleansing his people in the last days:

> "For I will take you from the nations, and gather you from all the countries, and bring you into your own land. I will dash clean water upon you and you shall be clean from all your uncleannesses, and from your idols I will cleanse you . . . and you . . . shall be my people, and I will be your God. And I will save you from all your uncleannesses" (Ezekiel 36:24-28).

Zechariah too saw this final time of national repentance: "There shall be a fountain opened to the house of David and to the inhabitants of Jerusalem for sin and uncleanness" (Zechariah 13:1).

Proselyte baptism washed the uncleanness from the heathen on entering Judaism. Thus non-Jews were grafted on to the people of God by a water immersion which gave them ceremonial purity. The Jewish prophet Yochanan Ha Mahtbeel

(John the Baptizer) called on all Israel to likewise admit sinful uncleanness and take a ritual bath "as a token of their repentance" (Mark 1:4) and resolve to keep themselves holy as they awaited the coming Messiah.

Then as the last days began to approach, the Jewish prophet Yochanan announced that the Messiah was on his way to pour out the Holy Spirit on some and the fire of judgment on others. Therefore, all men must turn from their own ways, look to God and his Messiah for mercy, be cleansed with clean water, and be saved from judgment (see Mark 1:4, Matthew 3:7, Luke 3:9).

Sensing by the Holy Spirit that the Messiah's presence on the earth was very near and that the need for preparing the Jewish people to meet their God had reached the crisis point, Yochanan Ha Mahtbeel called upon all his people to seek God's forgiveness by submitting to a purifying immersion bath. For this great Jewish prophet saw that the coming Messiah would judge the wicked who had not turned from the "Egyptian" evils of this world by taking a "Red Sea" immersion of separation and repentance in the Jordan River. God gave Yochanan (John) the foresight to see that those who did turn to God would be given the Holy Spirit by the Coming One, the Messiah.

Later John must have had inspired intimations of how God would save his people. John pointed to Yeshua and said, "Look, there is the Lamb of God; it is he who takes away the sin of the world. This is he of whom I spoke when I said, 'After me a man is coming whose status is higher than mine;' for before I was born, he already existed. I myself did not know who he was; but the very reason why I came, baptizing in water, was that he might be revealed to Israel" (John 1:29-31).

However, the immersion of John went beyond proselyte baptism in several ways. It was directed toward his fellow-Jews. It was a collective act of repentance and included the whole nation. It had a "last-chance" ethical and spiritual significance that went far beyond the mere ceremonial cleansing of proselyte baptism. John asserted that through his water ordeal the remnant of true spiritual Israel was being called out from all the spiritually dead who refused to prepare themselves by immersion for the coming of the Messiah. Therefore, all strata of Israel's society responded to the immersion of John, even the Sadducees and Pharisees (Matthew 3:5-7).

What was unique about John was that he saw by inspiration from the God of Israel that, in view of the coming of the Holy One, the Messiah, Jews were just as sinfully unclean as were proselytes, and must therefore prepare themselves by the same act of repentance — submitting to an immersion for the uncleanness of sins. John preached, "Do not presume to say to yourselves, 'We have Abraham for our father.' I tell you God can make children for Abraham out of these stones here" (Matthew 3:9). John knew that the essential thing for his fellow Jews was that they humble themselves, turn from prideful wickedness and prepare to adhere to the Messiah, through whom they would escape judgment and receive the all-important gift of God's Holy Spirit. Therefore, he saw that the whole nation of Israel must turn to God with the humility of a sinful non-Jew submitting to a mikveh of repentance for the sins of his unholy former life.

In pointing toward the Lamb of God, John pointed toward a new meaning for the mikveh bath as the standard means of making proselytes to Judaism. This new meaning would include a perfect blood sacrifice for sin, an eternal kaporrah for all who would receive the Holy Spirit and thus be circumcised as spiritual Jews through immersion in the name of the God of Israel. The mikveh bath toward which John was pointing was the immersion of Yeshua, experienced by Yeshua himself and then by him commanded for all peoples of the world.

THE IMMERSION OF THE JEWISH MESSIAH YESHUA

Yeshua's baptism was his first public act of identification with the sins of men, showing that although he was himself sinless, he was willing to identify with sinners and bear their sins as the Lamb of God, even if to do so would cost him his life.

When Yeshua went under the water in his own baptism, he knew he was anticipating his own death (see Luke 12:50). At his baptism, the heavenly voice of his Father (Mark 1:11, Matthew 3:17, Luke 3:22) affirmed Yeshua's Sonship but in words that alluded to his Messianic role (Psalm 2:7) in terms of suffering servanthood (Isaiah 42:1; 44:2) and death (Isaiah 53). Therefore, in his single action of being buried in water and rising again, Yeshua summed up and signified what he would do to save the world: he would bring in the new covenant of the Kingdom of God by his death, burial, and resurrection; and he would lead all who would follow him to a similar experience of death and new life — death to the old life of sin, and rebirth to a new life of eternal sonship through the gift of the Holy Spirit.

THE MIKVEH-BRIS OF THE SPIRITUAL JEW

✓ In Yeshua's immersion, he was submitting his own will in obedience to the will of his Father. When we likewise follow Yeshua into the water and have a similar spiritual experience of submitting our will to the Father, we are circumcised — that is, cleansed and consecrated — in our will by the Holy Spirit and thus become spiritual Jews.

Whereas before, our life was under the control of the law of sin and death (Romans 8:2), now our life comes under the Messiah. Therefore, it is not a rule that constrains us but a Person who loved sinners enough to die for us in order to forgive our past and bring us the hope of an eternal future with God (see II Corinthians 5:14). This Person is the Torah who writes himself upon our wills (Jeremiah 31:33). This inward life-giving law is none other than Yeshua (I Corinthians 9:21). Through the Holy Spirit, Yeshua lives in the lives of all believers and produces righteousness and love in communion with them. The selfless, Father-adoring love of the Son is what the Torah was aiming for (Deuteronomy 6:5), and when we receive the Word become Man, Yeshua, the law hits its mark in us and we become true Torah-keeping spiritual Jews whose wills are circumcised and born again by the Holy Spirit. For circumcision, the symbol of all law-keeping, is really a spiritual matter of the will and of love rather than pride in merit. To be a true Jew is to have the right heart toward God, and that can only be a heart of hopeful and loving faith (Galatians 5:6) in what God has done for men in Yeshua the Messiah.

Only the Word-become-Man who through the Holy Spirit becomes the Indwelling Word could endow men with a new principle of life. This principle of life is sufficient to create a new race of humanity (I Corinthians 15:20, 45; John 20:22), a new family of whom Yeshua is the head. To understand this "circumcision of Messiah" (Colossians 2:11), one must recall that the covenant of circumcision operated on the principle of the spiritual union of the household in its head.

The covenant is "between me and thee and thy offspring
after thee" (Genesis 17:7). From Galatians 3:16, 26-29, it
becomes apparent that both the offspring and head of the
new humanity is Messiah, into whose Body believers are
incorporated at their immersion.

Circumcision is the token or sign by which God acknowl-
edges his people. It is the stamp of the covenant. The circumcision of the heart is the inward sign wherein God's Spirit
witnesses to a human spirit that it belongs to God. This
inward mark of possession is the Holy Spirit who cuts himself
into our will, molding us into the image of God's Son and
marking us out as the spiritually cleansed property of God,
just as the external mark in the flesh (circumcision called a
bris) had marked out a Jewish baby boy as the property of
God.

But, as both the Torah and Tenach show, God intended to
"mark off" as his own not merely people who were circumcised physically but "in their hearts" (Deuteronomy 10:16).
So strong is this teaching, that God threatens to destroy any
Jew who is not spiritually circumcised (Jeremiah 4:4). Such
a one will be shut out of Jerusalem (Isaiah 52:1), as well
as the Lord's sanctuary (Ezekiel 44:7, 9) and salvation
(Deuteronomy 30:6). For not all God's physical people are
his spiritual children (Romans 9:6). In Genesis 17, circumcision is the covenant sign of God's choosing out and marking
off men for his own. So in the New Testament, the gift of the
Holy Spirit, without which a man does not belong to the
Messiah (Romans 8:9), is offered in connection with water
baptism (Acts 2:38), which is identified with Messiah's way
of circumcision (Colossians 2:11-12).

Jeremiah, the Jewish prophet, foresaw the age of the Holy
Spirit when the creation of a new heart and spirit in humanity
would be the essence of a new covenant that God would make
with Israel. Therefore, Jeremiah cried out to his people, "O
Jerusalem, wash thy heart from wickedness that thou may be
saved" (Jeremiah 4:14).

Water baptism is the rite of spiritual circumcision whereby
both Jews and Gentiles become spiritual Jews initiated into
covenant membership in Spiritual Israel. According to the
Torah, circumcision is more than a minor surgical operation —
it is also a major spiritual operation. The Torah commands,
"Circumcise the foreskin of your will and be no longer
stubborn . . . and the Lord your God will circumcise your

will (that is, cleanse and consecrate your will) . . . so that you will love the Lord your God with all your heart and with all your soul that you may live" (Deuteronomy 10:16; 30:6). In the Jewish New Covenant, God declares that you are not a true spiritual Jew unless you have this inward circumcision of your will (Romans 2:28, 29) and you worship him in spirit with your confidence in Yeshua Ha Mashiach and not in anything external (Philippians 3:3). Consequently, God has provided his people with a mikveh bath of purification whereby the impure foreskin of our evil urgings can be washed away by God's Holy Spirit (Ezekiel 36:25-27). This bath symbolizes both a spiritual mikveh (Jewish purification bath) and a spiritual bris (circumcision which makes one a Jew). It is sometimes called a mikveh-bris, and is a token of turning to God through faith in Yeshua.

There is a controlling sinful principle that exists in every man. The circumcision of the Messiah is the spiritual cutting away of this rebellious sinful nature as we are buried in water with him and will to die to our former sin-prone way of life. Only in this way may we be made alive by the resurrected, living Word of God, the Torah who came among us as a Man and wants to write himself upon our wills, as Jeremiah foresaw: "Then I will make a New Covenant with the house of Israel . . . I will put my Torah in their inward parts and I will write it in their hearts" (Jeremiah 31:31-34). Therefore, the mikveh-bris means many things. It is the cutting free of the downward pull of our lower natures. It is our Red Sea exodus from the bondage of sin and death to the inheritance of an eternal Promised Land. It symbolizes the "circumcision made without hands" whereby we become sons of the Covenant as we enter into faith-union with the Jewish Messiah as members of his bride, the world-wide fellowship of the Jewish New Covenant. Just as a Jewish girl takes the ritual bath of immersion in preparation for her wedding, so we who are wedded to Yeshua by faith take a mikveh to bring ourselves into union with him.

> "In him also you were circumcised, not in a physical sense, but by the stripping off of the lower nature; this is Messiah's way of circumcision. For in baptism you were buried with him, in baptism you were raised to life with him through your faith in the power of God who raised him from the dead. And although you were dead because of your sins and because you were morally uncircumcised, he has made you alive with Messiah" (Colossians 2:11-13).

THE MIKVEH-BRIS — YOUR ADMITTANCE
TO MESSIANIC JUDAISM'S COVENANT MEAL

"So long as a Gentile has not been immersed he is still a Gentile" (Ber. 288). Likewise, if a Jewish person has not taken the mikveh-bris, he is also ceremonially uncircumcised because he has not submitted to the ritual of spiritual circumcision which is the mikveh-bris of Messianic Judaism.

For, in the same way that a non-Jew coming up out of the water of his baptism was considered at that moment to be a Jew, ceremonially, when a person comes up from the mikveh of Yeshua he becomes a spiritual Jew.

The rabbis said that a proselyte was like one who had touched a corpse. Touching a corpse meant contracting seven days of uncleanness (Numbers 19:16). Therefore a proselyte, like a ritually unclean Israelite, needed to take an immersion in water as he approached God, particularly if he were to share in the Passover (see Mishnah Pesahim 8.8).

Likewise Rabbi Saul warned that those who eat and drink the Passover covenant meal of the Lord's Supper unworthily, without obeying the Lord (in this case by taking the mikveh), eat and drink judgment on themselves (I Corinthians 11:27-30). Therefore, no one may partake of the New Covenant Passover of the Lord's Supper until he has obeyed the Lord by submitting in repentance to the mikveh-bris.

Jewish proselyte baptism has its roots in the levitical immersions of the Torah (see Numbers 19). These purification baths were for ritually unclean Israelites who had defiled themselves by touching a corpse or other taboo object. Both pagans and ritually unclean Israelites were excluded from the Passover, because both were ritually unclean, one because he was not circumcised and baptized, the other because he had not taken a mikveh bath to remove his ceremonial uncleanness, and neither, of course, had the sacrifice commanded by the Torah (see Leviticus 15:13-25). A sacrifice was required of both pagans becoming Jews and unclean Israelites, and was offered by both after they took their water immersions.

Therefore, in order to gain entrance to the covenant meal of the Passover Seder, the same three conditions were required of proselytes as natural born, yet ceremonially unclean Jews. These three conditions were circumcision (required on the eighth day of the life of a natural born Jew), water immersion, and sacrifice. (See the reference to ritual immersions — the

23

prototype of water baptism — in the Torah: Leviticus 15:13; Numbers 8:7-8; Leviticus 14:1-32.)

In the Jewish New Covenant Scriptures, as we have seen, none of these three aspects of incorporation into the people of God is omitted. For where there is faith, water immersion into Messianic Judaism in the name of the God of Israel includes an eternal (spiritual) circumcision (Colossians 2:11-13), an eternal (spiritual) purification bath (Titus 3:5), and a perfect, eternal blood sacrifice for sin (Hebrews 9:12). Only those spiritual Jews who have covenanted themselves to the Lord Yeshua in the mikveh may sit at the table of Spiritual Israel and partake of the Passover covenant meal of the Lord's Supper.

THE MIKVEH-BRIS — AN ETHICAL IMPERATIVE FROM THE GOD OF ISRAEL

✓ Taking or not taking the mikveh-bris is really not an option, for the decision means obedience or disobedience to a divine command from the God of Abraham, Isaac, and Jacob. And who would argue with the risen Lord Yeshua, God's mighty Word come among us as an indestructible man? Certainly not the first adherents of Messianic Judaism, for, upon his authority, several thousand Messianic Jews were baptized within the first few weeks after the resurrection and ascension of Lord Yeshua.

Just as Gentiles had to get into the water to commit themselves to Judaism, so now that the Messiah has come and is coming again, everyone must get into the water and personally commit himself to Yeshua in order to remain in the mainstream of true Biblical Judaism. Where there is no true adherence to the Messiah of Judaism, there is no true adherence to Judaism. Anyone who refuses to take the mikveh-bris of Yeshua automatically removes himself from true Biblical Judaism, for as the Talmud does not fail to notice, "The world was only created for the Messiah" (Sanhedrin 98b) and "All the prophets prophesied of nothing but the days of the Messiah" (Sanhedrin 99a).

Some believers have had their spiritual life seriously stunted because they were hesitant to obey the Lord Yeshua by taking the mikveh. Others have suddenly become sick and had much satanic attack all because they refused to obey the Lord and take the mikveh. If you have prayed to receive

Yeshua, but have not yet taken the mikveh, and are consequently sick or feel no sense of blessing or nearness to God, now you know why. If you want blessed, read what Yeshua says to do: "Anyone who loves me will obey what I say; then my Father will love him, and we will come to him and live within him" (John 14:23).

Taking the mikveh is no magic insurance policy freeing people to live as they please without thought of the consequences. Taking the mikveh is a moral matter, and it means coming under the ethical direction and control of the Jewish Messiah Yeshua. To live otherwise is to make a mockery of one's mikveh-bris. To refuse to take the mikveh is in fact unethical behavior since it is disobedience of a command of the God of Israel and his Messiah (see Matthew 28:19).

The spiritual Jew spends the rest of his life working out the implications of his mikveh-bris and what it means spiritually and ethically to be living a life under the control of Messiah Yeshua. Without the intention of such a vital faith, the ceremony of the mikveh-bris is empty and meaningless.

Yeshua saves us through the *tebilah* (immersion) "of rebirth and renewing of the Holy Spirit" (Titus 3:5), as we "are born from water and the Spirit" (John 3:5). This does not mean that anyone who has not been baptized is automatically going to hell, but it does mean that anyone who says that he believes in Yeshua and yet refuses to submit to the mikveh-bris is in danger of coming under the judgment of the word of God: "The man who says 'I know him,' while he disobeys his commands, is a liar and a stranger to the truth" (I John 2:4). Yeshua commanded, "Baptize men everywhere in the name of the Father and the Son and the Holy Spirit and teach them to observe all that I have commanded you" (Matthew 28:19).

God wants to drown your sins just like he drowned those sinners in Noah's time (I Peter 3:20). But the question is, do **you** want God to wash away your sins? God knows that if you do, you'll get into the water. If you refuse to get into the water, how do you plan on convincing God that you're serious about wanting him to forgive you and wash away your sins? Your token of repentance to convince both you and God that you are serious about wanting your sins forgiven and washed away is your mikveh.

Love is not mere lip service. Love is something you do. Your first expression of love for the Lord Yeshua when you become a believer is to take the mikveh-bris of water

25

immersion. But first you must ask yourself how much you love God. Is he worth getting wet over or not? Yeshua says, "If you love me you will obey my commandments" (John 14:15).

From the beginning days of the community of Messiah Yeshua, there was no time separation between believing and being baptized. Those who believed **immediately** sought the Jewish *tebilah* of Yeshua. There was no mystery as to what one could do if he sincerely desired to be saved from his sins: believe Yeshua and obey him through a mikveh which is a token of your faith and repentance. "And now why delay? Be baptized immediately, with invocation of his name, and wash away your sins" (Acts 22:16). There is no probation period of waiting between the inward moment of faith and the outward moment of obedience through submission to the mikveh. Let your old sinful life die **today** in a sea of death so that through the name of his Son, the Father can give you his Spirit to make you a new creation.

THE JEWISH MANNER OF IMMERSION

In Judaism, complete immersion for proselytes was absolutely necessary, so that every part of the body was touched by water. So too in Messianic Judaism, complete immersion is the Scriptural mode. We are to be **buried** in water (see Romans 6:4 and Colossians 2:12) with the Messiah so that we can be **resurrected** out of the water (see Acts 8:39 and Matthew 3:16) with him to walk in a new path of life as spiritual Jews.

Secret or private, unwitnessed immersions were not acknowledged in Judaism, nor are they in Messianic Judaism. Both the mikveh and the covenant Passover meal of the Lord's Supper are public and not private ceremonies.

"In the name of the Lord Yeshua" is a Biblical abbreviation for the full name of the one God of Israel. His complete name emerges in the fullness of revelation from the Jewish scriptures as the **one** name of The-Father-and-the-Son-and-the-Holy Spirit, into whose one name we are baptized in the mikveh-bris. At your mikveh-bris, you will have implanted on you the majestic and mighty name of God, which will make you his property and throw his protection over you to cover you with the blood of his Son and to seal you against the assaults of the Enemy. For at your mikveh-bris you will enter

26

into covenant with the God of Israel, and when you come up out of the water the Jewish New Covenant will begin for you (Jeremiah 31:31-34).

Therefore, men are not born spiritual Jews, even if their parents are Jewish. To become a spiritual Jew, one must be born again (John 3:3) "through the water of rebirth and the renewing power of the Holy Spirit" (Titus 3:5). Jesus said, "No one can enter the Kingdom of God without being born from water and spirit" (John 3:5). Thus infant baptism is a misunderstanding of the **spiritual** nature of the circumcision effected through a believer's baptism, because infant baptism omits the all-important matter of personal saving faith.

Therefore, immature children who do not comprehend who Yeshua is nor depend on him as their Lord should not take the mikveh until later when they come to faith. Only believers are to be baptized: "He that believeth and is baptized shall be saved" (Mark 16:16).

UNDERSTANDING WHAT WE MUST DO

We who are the *maggidim* (preachers) of Messianic Judaism teach the Messiah's people what Rabbi Saul told Governor Felix in Acts 24:25. We speak of 1) morals, 2) self-control, 3) the coming judgment, and also we speak of 4) repentance, 5) forgiveness, and 6) obedience.

1) We know we all sin and are powerless to live as we should (Romans 7:21-25).
2) We need to turn from trusting in ourselves and receive the Holy Spirit in order to have the power to live as we should, both now and hereafter.
3) The Holy Spirit is given only in obedience to Lord Yeshua, who will judge all those who reject him, and who commands that our first act of obedience be to take a mikveh in the name of the God of Israel.
4) Repentance means deciding to live as **God** pleases rather than ourselves — and according to his Word. WILL YOU REPENT?
5) Forgiveness doesn't mean letting sinners off scot-free. God would be unrighteous if he did not decree just punishment for sin. Therefore, God could forgive us only if he took our punishment out on himself, on

part of himself that he sent among us as a man named
Yeshua. To be forgiven we must believe that God
took our punishment in this way, because God cannot
extend mercy at the expense of his justice. The
Messiah's death was in order that the Father could
righteously forgive all sin, since through the death of
the Son, no sins had gone unpunished. **DO YOU
BELIEVE THAT GOD CAN JUSTLY FORGIVE
YOUR SINS ONLY THROUGH THE PUNISHMENT
OF YESHUA?**

6) Obeying a traffic cop means obeying his hands. In the
    same way that **one** traffic cop can still have **two** hands,
    God our Father can have his Holy Spirit and his Living
    Word (Yeshua) and still be **one** God. Yeshua has
    proven that he is both God and Messiah by overcom-
    ing death. Now he demands that we obey him as the
    Lord and Master of our lives, doing whatever he
    commands in the Jewish Old or New Covenant
    Scriptures. **ARE YOU WILLING TO OBEY YESHUA
    AS THE DIVINE LORD AND MASTER OF YOUR
    LIFE?**

Here is a prayer which you can pray:

*God of Abraham, Isaac, and Jacob. I am a Jew
and I'm going to die a Jew. But I've decided
to stop living as I please. I promise to live by
your Word in both the Old and the New
Testaments. Father, I know that you can forgive my sins only through the punishment of
Yeshua. Yeshua, I believe that you overcame
death to prove that you are part of God, my
Messiah and my Lord. Come into my life.
Forgive my sins. Take control of my life. And
I'll obey you forever.*
                    In Yeshua's name, amen.

Are you willing to pray that prayer and mean it? Come to
our Messianic Synagogue on the last Sunday of the month.
Then join other Jewish believers in Yeshua who are obeying
him as Lord by submitting humbly to a mikveh of repentance
in the name of the God of Israel. On that day you should
arrive early in order to receive instructions on the significance
of this most meaningful Jewish ceremony. You should wear
clothes you don't mind getting wet and you should bring a
towel and a change of clothes. After you have obeyed the

Lord Yeshua in this simple and yet most beautiful and blessed of ceremonies you will be able to go with the other Jewish believers to celebrate the Passover covenant meal of the Lord's Supper which will occur in the Sunday morning service.

Acts 2:41-42 explains what the Lord Yeshua requires of his disciples: "And those who accepted the gospel took the mikveh-bris of water baptism, and they met persistently to hear the apostolic teaching, to have fellowship, to celebrate the Lord's Seder, and to pray." The Lord Yeshua commands that we take the mikveh-bris, that we partake of the Lord's Seder regularly (on Acts 2:42 Sunday, which is the last Sunday of each month) and that we attend believers' meetings faithfully.

We can still observe our Jewish customs after accepting Yeshua in our mikveh. The mikveh is not the end of our Jewishness. It is the true spiritual beginning of our Jewishness, the moment when the Jewish New Covenant becomes a reality in our life (see Jeremiah 31:31-34). In fact, we discover that after we obey Yeshua and become enlightened by the Holy Spirit, we are able to see more to appreciate in our Jewish customs and ceremonies that we ever believed possible.

SUMMARY

No respected modern scholar doubts the Jewish origin of the rite of water immersion. Historically, water immersion has been the indispensible ritual for all who would become adherents of Messianic Judaism.

The mission of Yeshua did not arise in a vacuum. It received the legacy of the zealous Jewish proselyting movement, to which it added the world-shaking power of the Holy Spirit in order to make more proselytes to Messianic Judaism than anyone ever dreamed possible. Judaism was carried to all peoples, Jews and Gentiles alike, by the followers of Yeshua. For Yeshua baptized Judaism with the Holy Spirit and brought God's people the Good News of the Kingdom which Judaism had for so long been waiting to take to the world.

Messianic Judaism has been given a world-wide commission by Yeshua, the risen Lord of Israel, to make all peoples proselytes to him and Messianic Judaism through the mikveh-bris. In this way God is calling out a people from all nations who, regardless of their culture, can become born-again spiritual Jews and eternal citizens of the Kingdom of God.

The door to Messianic Judaism is repentance and faith in the risen Lord Yeshua, expressed outwardly through a mikveh-bris of water immersion. In the same way that a non-Jew could be cleansed from sin and made a partaker of all the blessings of the covenant with Israel through proselyte baptism, now **all** peoples must become adherents to the Messiah of Messianic Judaism in order to enter into the new life of the Messianic age. Therefore, everyone — regardless of race or culture — must become a spiritual Jew through the inward reception of the Lord Yeshua outwardly expressed by submission to the mikveh-bris. The mikveh-bris is the rite of entry into the community of the Jewish Messiah, and this Messianic community is concretely symbolized by the Passover covenant meal of the Lord's Supper. Only those who have covenanted themselves to the Lord Yeshua by obeying him in the mikveh may partake of his Passover covenant meal, the Lord's Supper.

Once Yeshua appeared and Messianic Judaism focused on him as its continuing center, all Jews, in order to remain in the mainstream of Messianic Judaism, had to stop relying on their own merit and had to submit to a mikveh themselves in order to adhere to the true Messianic faith of their fathers.

When God the Father pinpointed his identity through the particular Jew Yeshua, his Son, anyone refusing to pay homage to Yeshua did not know nor worship the true God of Israel (John 5:23, Luke 10:22). Moreover, to refuse to take the mikveh is in fact unethical since it is disobedience to a command of the God of Israel and his Messiah.

The mikveh-bris is our glad response to the Good News of Messianic Judaism. It is our obedient dying to our old life of sin, so that we can arise with the Messiah to a new abundant life as spiritual Jews.

NOTE: *We'd like you to return this valuable second document. However, when you take the mikveh-bris, we have a third document for you. You'll receive it on Acts 2:42 Sunday, the last Sunday of the month, if you are willing to take the mikveh-bris at that time.*

Part Three

The Cost of Commitment in Messianic Judaism

Contents

THE COST OF COMMITMENT IN MESSIANIC JUDAISM

*These page numbers refer to those at the top.

III

Counting the Cost before Your Mikveh-Bris

You are getting ready to seal the contract between yourself and the God of your fathers, who on this day of your immersion is making you a party eligible for the privileges and responsibilities of the Jewish New Covenant.

THE PRIVILEGE OF BECOMING GOD'S COVENANT PROPERTY

When you are submerged into the water in the name of the God of Israel — the name of the Father and the Son and the Holy Spirit — this means that you are being dedicated in this one name fo the one God of Israel whose property you now become. You are now no longer your own, you have been purchased at great price, at the cost of the blood of the Lamb of God, Yeshua Ha Mashiach.

By your act of submitting to Yeshua's will in the mikveh-bris, you are confessing your faith that Yeshua is your Messiah and your Lord.

The mikveh-bris is a time when the Spirit of the God of Israel creates a new vitality in the believer's life. For in baptism the believer gratefully submits his will to the Spirit of God, realizing that God loves us so much that he has appeased his holy wrath at our sin by taking his anger out on himself, on part of his own being, on his Son — rather than on us who deserve it. The death of God the Son in your place and the revelation of God's eternal life through Yeshua's resurrection from the dead is God's gift of infinite love to you in order that he might give you life.

If you accept his Son as Lord and confess Yeshua as both God and Master of your life, you thereby renounce your **own** sin-prone will and resolve to live by **his** holy will as it is recorded for you in the Old and New Covenant Jewish

Scriptures. Therefore, the reason you get into the water is quite simple: the divine Lord Yeshua Ha Mashiach **commands** you to submit to the mikveh-bris and you dare not disobey him. In fact, it is as you **do** obey him that you know that Yeshua is **your** Lord. This knowledge is joy unspeakable, the joy of your new birth and the salvation of your soul.

Stepping into the water in obedient faith to Lord Yeshua, you are cut free from the downward pull of your old nature and spiritually circumcised by the Holy Spirit as your sins are drowned and buried in the water. When you are raised out of the water you joyfully believe God's promise that your life is now privileged to be under the control of the Son of God through the Spirit of God, and you can now begin to live in the newness of life as a spiritual Jew and an eternal son of God.

A SERIOUS DECISION

However, there is something for you to stop and consider first. The Scriptures teach that although many of the Jewish people believed in Yeshua, some refused to become his disciples (students), because they feared their own people and because they valued their reputation with men more than they valued the honor that comes from God. You should count the cost of becoming a disciple before you publicly accept Yeshua as your Lord in the mikveh-bris.

WHAT YOUR LORD YESHUA WILL COMMAND

The Scriptures plainly teach what Yeshua commands of you as his disciple:
1) that you decide to obey God's Word and to be immersed in the name of the Father, Son, and Holy Spirit (Acts 2:38; Matthew 28:19);
2) that you not stay away from believers' meetings but remain a faithful and regular student of apostolic teaching (Acts 2:42);
3) that you stay in regular fellowship with other believers (Hebrews 10:25);
4) that you be a regular partaker of the Lord's Seder (Acts 2:42);
5) that you remain faithful in corporate and private prayer (Acts 2:42);
6) that you submit to the pastoral counsel of one body

34

of believers (Hebrews 13:17);
7)   that you faithfully focus your financial giving, talents, and spiritual gifts in one body of believers (Malachi 3:10; Acts 4:35; I Corinthians 14:26);
8)   that you as a disciple make disciples (John 15:8).

HOW MUCH IS YESHUA WORTH TO YOU?

Furthermore, the Lord Yeshua Ha Mashiach commands that his disciples put him above everyone and everything else in the world, including your family, your possessions, and even your own life (Luke 14:25-33). When you step into the immersion waters you are walking into potential martyrdom. Your family may disown you and you may suffer great loss and persecution. You must count the cost.

Rabbi Saul, who was persecuted greatly and died a martyr, wrote:

> "But all is far-outweighed by the gain of knowing Messiah Yeshua my Lord, for whose sake I did in fact lose everything . . . All I care about is to know Messiah, to experience the power of his resurrection, and to share his sufferings, in growing conformity with his death, if only I may finally arrive at the resurrection from the dead" (Philippians 3:8,11). *(NEB)*

WOULD-BE FOLLOWERS

Lord Yeshua warned that some would-be disciples, not counting the cost, would seemingly receive the Word with joy, but it would strike no root in them; they'd have no staying power; then, when there is trouble or persecution on account of the Word, they'd fall away at once. Others also would hear the Word, but worldly concerns and the false glamor of wealth and all kinds of evil desire would come in and choke the Word and it would prove barren (Mark 4). Take John the Baptist's warning: "There is no use being baptized without a true and lasting decision that shows itself in actions" (Luke 3:8).

NO LOOKING BACK

The Scriptures also warn, "When men have once been enlightened, when they have had a taste of the heavenly gift and a share in the Holy Spirit, when they have experienced the good Word of God and the spiritual energies of the age

35

to come, and after this have fallen away, it is impossible to bring them again to repentance; for with their own hands they are killing the Son of God again and making mock of his death" (Hebrews 6:4-6). This passage means that we must approach our immersion with the utmost seriousness and never look back on it lightly as though the commitment it symbolizes is something to trifle with! Count the cost! Yeshua warns, "No one who sets his hand to the plow and then keeps looking back is fit for the kingdom of God. If you love me you will obey my commandments" (Luke 9:62; John 14:15). *(NEB)*

WHAT NEXT?

Now, since immersion is the door to the *chavaroot* (fellowship) of believers in Yeshua and since you obviously believe that God has sent you to our Messianic Synagogue to be immersed, then you should assume that the Lord wishes you to commit yourself to the Body of believers at our Messianic Synagogue, unless you are Scripturally, prayerfully prompted otherwise. In order that you may be able to be received into membership by next "Acts 2:42 Sunday," the last Lord's Day of next month, we are making available for your prayerful consideration and signature the following: 1) the membership application, 2) the information sheet, and 3) an envelope for your forwarding this material to us as promptly as possible. When we receive these materials from you, if you are to be received as a member, it will be on the last Lord's Day of that same month. At that time new members will receive their membership manuals. In connection with your decision, take with you and read this week the document entitled "The Jewish Life of Discipleship" which we have included with your application for membership.

We of our Messianic Synagogue urge you to approach your mikveh-bris with seriousness but also with real expectancy and excitement. Your immersion should be a time of blessing for you as well as a time when you can look to the Lord for direction in how he would have you serve him. Therefore, approach your immersion with the same joyful hope that you should always have when you step out in faith to obey the Word of God.

Just as Yeshua experienced his call to service from his Father at his own immersion, so too you should see this as the time when God formally enlists and authorizes you to be a servant of his divine Son, and obligates himself to be your protector and loving benefactor.

When you come up out of the water you are at that moment a son of God (Romans 8:14-17), a recipient of the blessings of the New Covenant (Jeremiah 31:31-34), a spiritual child of Abraham by faith (Galatians 3:7), and a spiritual (and therefore true) Jew (Romans 2:28-29). If there ever was a time when you should raise your hands and praise the God of Israel, it is when you come up out of the water! Baruch ha shem! May God's richest blessing rest on you all the days of your life!

Scriptures for study: Colossians 2:11-13; Romans 2:28-29; Acts 2:38; Romans 6:1-11; Romans 8:14-17.

Synagogue
Membership Application

I, _____, trusting Yeshua as my
kaporrah and personal Messiah and the divine Son of God,
wish to become a member of this Messianic Synagogue. As a
baptized Jewish disciple of Yeshua, I promise to faithfully
continue in the apostolic teaching, the *chavaroot* (fellowship),
the Lord's Seder, and prayer (Acts 2:42) of this synagogue. I
also promise to humbly submit to the spiritual leadership of
this synagogue, accepting correction in the same spirit of love
in which it is given (Hebrews 13:17), since I realize these
leaders "must render an account for me." I furthermore
agree to obey Malachi 3:8-10 and I pledge to support this
synagogue not only with my financial giving, but my talents,
my time, and my spiritual gifts in order to do all that I can to
win disciples to this Body of Yeshua in our local Jewish
community.

In Yeshua's name
And for his glory,

Signed_____

Date_____

NOTE: If you complete this application for membership, turn
or mail it in with the information sheet (on the reverse) filled
out, so that it can be processed in time for you to receive
membership and your manual by next Acts 2:42 Sunday,
the last Lord's Day of next month.

INFORMATION SHEET FOR MEMBERS
OF OUR MESSIANIC SYNAGOGUE

Family Name _____ Date _____

Husband_____ Wife _____

Birthday_____ Birthday_____

Child _____ Child _____
            Birthdate   Birthdate

Child _____ Child _____
            Birthdate   Birthdate

Address _____

City _____ Zip_____

Phone_____

In case of emergency, please list your business address and number:

Husband's Business _____

Wife's Business_____

Religious Background _____

Do you have relatives in our Messianic Synagogue? If so, please list their names:

_____

YOU WANT TO USE YOUR "GIFTS" FOR FELLOWSHIP MINISTRY IN THE FOLLOWING AREAS:

Phone Ministry _____ Bus Ministry _____

Teaching _____ What age group?_____ Experience? _____

Faith sharing _____ Membership visitation work_____

Stewardship committee _____ Nursery _____

Music _____ Singing? _____ What instruments? _____

Office work _____ Hours weekly? _____ Special abilities_____

Youth ministry_____Of what sort? _____

Other _____

NOTE: COMPLETE THIS FORM AND TURN OR MAIL IT IN WITH YOUR APPLICATION FOR MEMBERSHIP.

The Jewish Life of Discipleship

The Hebrew word *chavair* means "friend." *Chavaroot* means "fellowship." That a disciple could be his master's *chavair* or friend was unheard of at the time of Yeshua, for then a disciple was to keep a respectful distance from his master, adhering to him with only the abashed formality of a slave.

SLAVES BECOME GOD'S FRIENDS

Rabbi Joshua ben Levi asserted that a disciple could do anything for his master that a slave could do, except take off his shoes (Bab. Ket. 96a). John the Baptist said he was not worthy even to do that for Yeshua (see Matthew 3:11). A Jewish disciple at that time was expected to have a devotion to his master comparable to that of a slave, freely yoking himself to his master's service.

However, Yeshua elevated the disciple's devotion to a new level. He says, "You are my *chavarim*, my friends, if you do what I command you. I call you slaves no longer; a slave does not know what his master is about. I have called you friends, because I have disclosed to you everything that I heard from my Father" (John 15:14-15).

The best Hebrew word to describe these intimate meetings that Yeshua had with his immediate disciples is *chavaroot* or fellowship. There is a long standing Jewish custom for friends to meet for the purpose of table fellowship and social-religious discussion and prayer, not only on erev Shabbat (Sabbath eve), but at other occasions as well. Any group of friends that met consistently on a weekly basis for such intimate sharing was called a *chaburah*.

41

FELLOWSHIP WITH GOD

What was unique about the *chavaroot* of Yeshua was that through such fellowship the disciples were raised to a new intimacy with God, becoming (like Abraham) God's friends, and experiencing through the Holy Spirit, God's eternal resurrection life revealed through his Son. It was in just such a setting of table fellowship that the Risen Lord Yeshua appeared to his frightened disciples and they fellowshipped with God himself!

And here the proof that the Son is God was given in his resurrection, which was much more than a dead man seen alive. Yeshua's resurrection was the eternal life of God bodily visible to God's friends. With the resurrection of Yeshua, who was both God and man, the promised Resurrection unto eternal life has **already** begun, for the first man has already stepped out of the grave and all that is left is for the redeemed to follow. Moreover, now that he has resurrected and ascended, the Son of God has been exalted to Lordship. Yeshua is Lord. This is the confession without which there is no salvation (Romans 10:9). Yeshua is Lord in the sense that he is both God and Master of our lives. As Lord, Yeshua has poured out the Spirit (Acts 2:33), Yeshua has become the object of faith (Acts 2:21, 3:16), Yeshua is the Holy One (Acts 3:14), Yeshua is the author of life (Acts 3:15), and Yeshua will be the judge of the world (Acts 10:42).

We must remember the holiness of Yeshua. The Messiah of Israel is divine (see Isaiah 9:6). Yeshua is God. Not God the Father but God the Son. We are all sons of God but only Yeshua is God's **own** Son, who has always been part of his very being, even before Yeshua came among us as a man. We must remember that it was through the Son that the Father created the world. None of us is the Son of God in that sense. The Son is God, we are the Son's creation.

But we depend on God's Son not only for having created us, but also for revealing the Father to us. We know the Father only because we know the Son (Luke 10:22). Therefore, the fellowship of the first Jewish believers in Yeshua was unparalleled in human history. It was a fellowship in which the Father was intimately and personally known as never before. It was a fellowship in which the Father was present through his risen divine Son (at first visibly, later invisibly). It was a fellowship in which the miraculous healing

42

powers of the age to come were present by means of the
Holy Spirit. In brief, it was a fellowship in Yeshua's resurrection life, experienced in all but its future perfection right
now in the present age (see I John 1:1-4). Therefore, to be a
disciple is to experience the new life of the new age even **now**
in our joyful fellowship with God and with one another.

WHY MEET ON SUNDAY?

Because the Lord Yeshua first resurrected and appeared to
his disciples on Sunday (John 20:1), and appeared to them
again the following week on Sunday (John 20:26), finally
pouring out the Holy Spirit on them (Acts 2:1) on Sunday
(Shavuos A.D. 30), Sunday became known as the Lord's Day.
Thus it became an established Jewish tradition to meet on
the Lord's Day for *chavaroot*.

It was not enough for Jewish people to witness to the fact
that God rested on the seventh day after the creation. It was
now necessary also to witness to the fact that God worked
a new eternal creation on the eighth day, the first day of the
new creation, when his Son resurrected to become the head
of a new eternal humanity who are experiencing their new
life of fellowship in him already, even in this dying world in
advance of the age to come. Therefore, the first Jewish
believers did not fail to acknowledge both the Sabbath and
the Lord's Day. This is why it is so important for Messianic
Judaism that Jewish disciples meet for services on both Friday
night and Sunday, preserving Saturday for a family day of
rest. By meeting on both Friday night and Sunday, Jewish
believers point to the continuity of their Jewish faith, preserving both its past and its future as they witness to the
fullness of their Judaism for the benefit of the salvation of
their local Jewish community.

NO MATURITY WITHOUT COMMITMENT

The Biblical pattern for a body of believers such as our
Messianic Synagogue is that we be an expression of Messiah
Yeshua, representing him locally among our people in the
Jewish community. God has designed that each believer in
Yeshua be personally committed to a particular assembly or
synagogue (which is the Greek word for "assembly" — see
James 2:2). This is because we have a team responsibility to

help one another grow in spiritual maturity and in usefulness for the service of God, without which we cannot render adequate worship.

PUNCH ONLY ONE CLOCK

In the first place, commitment to one local assembly is the New Covenant pattern. As we open the Bible and read Acts and the epistles it is evident that believers are in submission to one specific local body. The Jewish believers who set the world on fire for God 2000 years ago were not running around from meeting hall to meeting hall. They were committed to one meeting hall and were putting their full strength in one synagogue, rather than scattering and diluting their energies in several directions. Because they obeyed God and combined their talents and skills and financial and spiritual resources in localized team efforts, these Jewish believers had an impact in every community where they lived.

Have you ever tried to work in two or three places of employment at one time? If you have, you know that by spreading yourself thin you don't do your best at any job. If you want to succeed in the business world you have to have one place where you focus all your concentration with one team of people. Moonlighting here and there is just going to wear you out and you're not really going to do anybody any good. It's the same working for the Kingdom of God. You can't punch the clock in three different congregations and get anything done for Yeshua. And if you spread your tithe around instead of focusing it in one assembly as the Lord commands (Malachi 3:8-10), your disobedience dissipates the purchasing strength of your own financial resources. The Biblical mandate is that we submit ourselves, our tithes, and our time to one body and no more.

LISTEN TO ONLY ONE SHEPHERD

Secondly, the Bible teaches that someday the Pastor or Shepherd of each flock is going to have to give an accounting for each believer for whom he has been responsible. As undershepherds of the Great Shepherd Yeshua, these men will stand before our Messiah and render an account (Hebrews 13:17). Now this should make us realize that every believer must have a shepherd. The Jewish Scriptures teach, "I will give you shepherds according to my will, which shall feed you with knowledge and understanding" (Jeremiah 3:15). If you do not have a shepherd or pastor who is responsible to Yeshua for you, then how are you yourself going to stand before God guiltless? There are those that run from meeting hall to meeting hall on the supposition that they have a pastor or pastors to whom they are in submission. However, in reality these people are in submission to nobody but themselves and are willfully disobedient to God's Word, which commands them to meet regularly together in one body (Hebrews 10:25) and to celebrate the Lord's Seder regularly (I Corinthians 11:24; Acts 2:42) together. Therefore, as a believer you have the responsibility to adhere to a spiritual shepherd and to throw your strength into that flock alone.

Did you ever hear of a sheep belonging to three or four different flocks? What a traumatic and confusing experience for any animal! How could such a freakish sheep be sure of his steps or avoid getting lost? Such wandering sheep would be smart to stop listening to themselves and start listening to what the Great Shepherd has to say in his Word.

DEVELOP YOUR GIFTS IN ONE BODY

Thirdly, we need to realize that God has given to each believer certain spiritual gifts. However, in many cases these gifts are latent in an individual without his being aware of them, because he has never been committed to any one body long enough to exercise them. But the Lord expects each one of us to use the gifts that he has invested in us. We have the responsibility to locate in an atmosphere where we can systematically grow and mature and our gifts can come to their full expression.

Do you know what your gifts are and are you **using** them in **one** body now where they will serve the Kingdom of God and reach our Jewish people? One of the reasons God has formed the body of our Messianic Synagogue is that many of our people could not properly exercise their gifts because they were uncommitted and uninvolved. But now every believer, including you, has the opportunity and the responsibility to use his gifts for the glory of God. And if you are Jewish, we offer you the unique challenge of using your gifts in a body that is an expression of Yeshua Ha Mashiach

in our local Jewish community in order that our people might
be saved.

GET RESPONSIBLE

Fourthly, the Bible teaches that just as a body cannot
accomplish anything without its various members functioning
in coordination, so too is the Body of Yeshua. Without hands,
fingers can't feed a mouth. Both our Messianic Synagogue and
the unsaved Jewish community at large are suffering the loss
of your hands. We need, and the Lord demands, that we have
the undiluted spiritual and financial strength of all those who
would join with us. Are you dead-serious about reaching our
Jewish people for Yeshua? Ask yourself the question: "Am I
giving my maximum time and finances and talents for reaching
our people? Or do I run around a lot and give only a little bit
here and a little bit there?" This question will be a very relevant
one when we all stand before the judgment seat of Yeshua
and give an accounting of our time and money and obedience
to Hebrews 13:17 and Malachi 3:8-10.

There is a price to pay for disobedience, even for believers.
We either obey the Lord and do our best to serve him, giving
him quality service as we build for him with the highest
standards of which we are capable, or we pay later.

> "If anyone builds on the foundation (of Messiah Yeshua)
> with gold, silver, and fine stone, or with wood, hay and
> straw, the work that each man does will at last be brought
> to light; the day of judgment will expose it. For that day
> dawns in fire, and the fire will test the worth of each
> man's work. If a man's building stands, he will be re-
> warded; if it burns he will have to bear the loss; and
> yet he will escape with his life as one might run from
> a fire" (I Corinthians 3:12-15). *(NEB)*

Therefore, the question is not if you will tie into a body
but **where** you will tie in, because there really is no option
in this matter. We defy God at our own risk. Judaism has
never been a philosophy, though some have tried to see
it in the pagan light of Greece. Judaism is a revealed religion
which does not ask for philosophic opinion, but rather
demands obedience from all men to God and to his
Messiah. The Lord says, "Obey your leaders" (Hebrews 13:17),
and this doesn't mean tipping your hat respectfully from
shepherd to shepherd as you wander from flock to flock.
This means joining one flock and listening to one pastor.

46

HANG IN HERE

We of our Messianic Synagogue are one of the very few effective expressions of Yeshua Ha Mashiach in the Jewish community. We are prayerfully asking God to give us you. If you come with us, you will not be joining a choir of angels; we are just redeemed sinners trying but not always succeeding to grow up to the full stature of Yeshua. However, the longer we put up with one another and try to love one another despite our faults, the more we grow to love like Yeshua loves and the more we become like him. Therefore, don't expect too much from us and don't run out the door the first time our behavior disappoints you. Instead, stay and ask Yeshua to help you love our unloveliness and you'll grow in your ability to be compassionate and tolerant.

It is our prayer that you will sign the application for membership and fill out the information sheet and send them to our synagogue at once. Then, on the next Acts 2:42 Sunday, we will have the joy of offering you both the right hand of fellowship and our membership manual as you become an integral part of our synagogue.

Thus, locking arms together with you in the marvelous love of Yeshua and the supernatural life of the Holy Spirit, our synagogue will be able to reach out to our lost people before it's too late. For this is the Biblical pattern, that you be committed to one Body and one leader with your full resources focused in one place for the maximum glory of God to shine in a lost world.

NOTE: *Now that you've read this entire document we'd like you to return it. The next document you receive from us you will not return. It is our synagogue member's manual. You will receive it next Acts 2:42 Sunday, the last Sunday of the month, if you have taken the mikveh-bris and if your signed membership application has by then been turned in and processed.*

Part Four

A Messianic Synagogue
Member's Manual

Contents

A MESSIANIC SYNAGOGUE MEMBER'S MANUAL

*These page numbers refer to those at the top.

IV

The Good News and the Lord's Seder

The Passover comes from the Hebrew word *pesah*, which means "to pass over" in the sense of "to spare the life" (Exodus 12:13-17). God passed over the blood-sprinkled Israelite houses and spared their lives from the wrath he inflicted on the heathen Egyptians, who had neither blood sacrifice nor faith. It was the blood of the sacrificial victim, the lamb, placed on the lintels of the Israelite homes that effected their release from God's wrath. And thus the Passover Seder came to commemorate that blood-sprinkled exodus to freedom and new life which is the essence of the faith of Israel.

WHY WE NEED TO BE "PASSED OVER"

It's important to keep in mind that believers in Yeshua are also "passed over" — spared the wrath of God — in the Jewish New Covenant, just as they were in the Old Covenant. Unfortunately, many people do not know that the Last Supper took place in the context of a Passover feast. This New Covenant Passover Seder commemorated a new exodus of salvation effected by Yeshua's own death as he offered himself as the Lamb of God who takes away the sin of the world.

And believers at this New Covenant Seder table are in fact "passed over," saved to a new life of freedom. For the God of Israel is the Great Kinsman of his people who "bails them out" of captivity at great cost to himself because he loves them. Our wills were held captive by the sinful ways of this "Egyptian" world rather than the will of him who created us. In his mercy the God of Israel came to post the "bail-bond" of his Son's blood in exchange for our freedom and peace.

51

We stood legally condemned under a death-curse. Without obedient faith we had arrogantly presumed that our good deeds merited God's favor. But all our presumptuous efforts to impress God by our own goodness stand condemned, because the Torah teaches that all who proudly rely on their ability to render God perfect obedience are under a death-curse: "A curse upon any man who does not uphold everything that is written in the Book of the Law" (Deuteronomy 27:26). Truly righteous people rely on faith, not on their own merit (see Habakkuk 2:4). Because of our faithless disobedience, our arrogant independence from God, and our tendency to think of ourselves as better than we are, we deserve to die. Yet in his mercy the God of Israel sent part of himself, his own sinless Divine Son Yeshua to take that death-curse upon himself in exchange for our freedom **from** the death-curse. And because Yeshua paid the death penalty of divine judgment on our sins, his death purchased an actual, Torah-based freedom from the bondage of sin and its death-curse. Therefore, we who believe have been **bought** into the liberty of freedmen, no longer slaves of sin and guilt, but transformed, Holy Spirit-endowed sons of God.

Now, having been bailed out of the "Egyptian" captivity of our own sinful wills, we obediently live by the will of God's own Divine Son, who died for us in order that we might live for him. Therefore, we know to whom we belong and the great price it cost him to redeem us. This is why the New Covenant Passover Seder of the Lord's Supper — sometimes called the Lord's Seder — means so much to us.

THE MEANING OF THE BREAD AND WINE

In the Lord's Seder, under Yeshua's sovereign Word, the bread becomes his body yielded up in God's redeeming plan (see Hebrews 10:5-10). And his blood outpoured in death, recalling the sacrificial rites of the Old Covenant, is represented in the cup of blessing on the table. That cup is invested henceforward with a fresh significance as the memorial of the New Exodus accomplished at Jerusalem (see Luke 9:31) through his blood. Messiah's body, then, becomes the "bread of affliction" of the Passover table of the Jewish New Covenant.

Just as bread and wine were symbols of the divine peace that the high priest Melchizedek mediated to Abraham

(Genesis 14:18), so the Great High Priest Yeshua offers himself through the bread and wine as God's peace offering to men. His broken body and outpoured blood are the only acceptable peace terms to bring reconciliation between a just, holy God and sinful men. For without the infinite injury which the Father inflicted on the Son, God in all justice would have had to declare an eternal war in hell on all the sins of men. God's peace offering, the blood of the Lamb of God, is his only acceptable restitution for the sins of guilty, God-alienated men, and the Lord's Seder is the only real Peace Table in this world. The task of Messianic Judaism is to per-ᵛ suade men everywhere to submit to a mikveh of repentance so that they may gather around the Prince of Peace and be assured at his Seder table that they have been "passed over" and given the eternal peace of God. This means that all men must be persuaded to accept the Messiah of Israel as their King.

At the Lord's table, the fellowship of Spiritual Israel is gathered as the people of the New Covenant (Jeremiah 31:31-34), and is confronted afresh with the tokens of Yeshua's once-offered sacrifice in the form of a covenant meal. At this table the new people of God relive that experience by which they came out of the Egypt of sin and were ransomed to God by the precious death of the Lamb of God, Yeshua Ha Mashiach. The inner meaning of the Lord's Seder is sharing with the Lord himself in his death and risen life, signified by the bread and the wine. In this sharing, Spiritual Israel experiences her unity, partaking of the one loaf as the one body of the Jewish Messiah. In the unseen presence of the Lord at his table, Spiritual Israel has a foretaste of the glorious Messianic banquet in the New Jerusalem where we will sit with Moses and millions of other spiritual Jews in the age to come.

WHO MAY PARTAKE

Exodus 12:43-49 excludes Gentiles from participation in the Passover Seder. Likewise, the Lord's Seder, the Passover meal of the Jewish New Covenant, excludes spiritual Gentiles who have not yet become born-again spiritual Jews. To sit at the Lord's Seder table, one must be a spiritual Jew, circumcised of the will and the spirit, having undergone the rite of spiritual circumcision (the mikveh-bris), or one will be eating and drinking judgment on oneself (I Corinthians 11:29). Regardless of one's culture or race, one cannot partake of Spiritual Israel's covenant meal until one has personally covenanted himself to the Lord Yeshua by submitting to the mikveh-bris of water baptism.

The rite of the mikveh-bris is the symbol of spiritual death and spiritual resurrection. For baptism symbolizes the believer's union with Messiah through faith in which the believer dies to his sin-prone life and is raised to walk in the newness of life as a spiritual Jew. No one can celebrate the New Exodus from sin and death commemorated by the Lord's Seder unless that exodus has become a reality for him through his own spiritual circumcision, which faith confers and which the mikveh-bris confirms (see Colossians 2:11-13).

EATING AND DRINKING BECOME PREACHING

The Lord's Supper Jewishly observed has evangelistic power. For, when both baptism and the Lord's Supper are publicly and properly administered, with only baptized believers allowed to receive the Lord's Supper, the Lord's Supper becomes a corporate sermon (I Corinthians 11:26) calling men to make the faith response of water baptism in order that they too may be no more excluded from the Lord's Supper. For as I Corinthians 11:26 says, every time we eat this bread and drink this cup we are, by that very eating and drinking, preaching. We are preaching the saving significance of the Lord Yeshua's death, which is the chief task of Messianic Judaism until the Lord comes again. The Lord's Seder is a corporate sermon because when people, especially Jewish people, see that responding to the Gospel is a very Jewish thing to do because baptism is a mikveh-bris and the Lord's Supper is a Seder, then the tension is on them to confess Yeshua as Lord by getting into the water in order to be no more excluded from the Lord's Seder. For making disciples is drawing lines and persuading men to cross them. The Lord's Supper, properly administered, persuades men to cross the baptism line into discipleship.

In effect, then, when we partake of the Lord's Seder, we are celebrating our spiritual circumcision, our spiritual exodus and our actual water baptism that incorporated us into spiritual Israel. For in eating and drinking, we are celebrating our new life as spiritual Jews. And as we participate in the

Lord's Seder, by that very participation we are defining who we are: spiritual Israel. As a matter of fact, the Seder is itself visual proclamation in that it calls men to realize that they are either inside or outside the circle of spiritual Israel (and therefore salvation) and must make a decision to either remain outside spiritual Israel or (via baptism) to enter spiritual Israel and eat at Messiah's table. When men see the Lord's Seder celebrated, they must understand that a line is being drawn which they either cross or do not cross, depending on whether or not they will receive the Word of God. In the Lord's Seder, people are confronted with a choice: they can either remain "Egyptian", spiritual pagans and be left behind in the Egypt of this dying world, or they can respond to the Seder's proclamation and (via baptism) can sit with spiritual Israel and her Messiah and enter that pilgrimage and exodus upon which we as born-again, spiritual Jews have already embarked.

Therefore, preaching shares with immersion and the Lord's Seder for in all three ways the Word of God draws a line, confronting men with the decision to either cross that line or not cross it, get in the water or not get in the water, eat and drink or not eat and drink, become a spiritual Jew or remain a spiritual pagan. The Lord's Seder, then, is the time when we can eat and drink the Word, wilfully receiving it, or rather wilfully receiving him who is the Word, Yeshua Ha Mashiach. The heart of our life is in *chavaroot* (fellowship) with Messiah, but it is in the fellowship created by preaching, by a mikveh, and by a common Jewish meal of bread and wine. In the Lord's Seder we have a foretaste of the bread of heaven here on earth as we also have that same foretaste in the Word of God as it is verbally proclaimed in preaching. Preachers need to understand the Jewishness of their role, functioning as they do as Moses-figures who call people out of Egypt into a new exodus of salvation and offer them the opportunity to exit death and sin via a red sea of water immersion and a seder table of salvation. Gentile preachers who are ignorant of the Jewishness of their task blur the definition of what the church is in relation to Israel, what the Jewish New Covenant Scriptures are in relation to the Jewish Old Covenant Scriptures, and they blur this not only for Jews who have traditionally been unresponsive to the proclamation of the Church and have not seen the relevance of it, but they also miss the significance for Gentiles. For a Christian can only know who he is himself when he understands who he is in relation to the Jews at whose table he is eating.

THE MESSAGE WE PREACH

According to the Hebrew prophets, the Holy Spirit would be given to men to write the will of God — the "Torah" — on their hearts (Jeremiah 31:33; Ezekiel 36:26-27). Thus the law in the New Covenant is not merely a written external code but an inward life-giving power that produces righteousness and is ceremonially received in the mikveh-bris. This inward life-giving law is none other than Yeshua. Through the Holy Spirit, Yeshua lives in the lives of all believers and produces righteousness and love in communion with them.

✓Yeshua is the mediator of the promised New Covenant of Jeremiah 31:31-34. Yeshua brings cleansing of sin and consecration to a new people of God whose endowment of the Holy Spirit gives them power over sin to obey God. Yeshua's blood is his sacrificial death which was made to pay for the forgiveness of our sins and to appease the wrath of God against us and to avert God's hatred of our unrighteousness. The Son is the Father's gift of love to us that he might give us life. For Messiah, by his atoning death, has done away with the enmity between a Holy God and sinful death-deserving men, bringing about a comprehensive peace which includes complete wholeness spiritually and a right relationship with God issuing in right relations with our fellow men. We can make peace with others only because God has made peace with us: he has sent part of his very being to take on flesh in the womb of an unmarried woman or virgin (Isaiah 7:14) in order to die for us that he might share with us his inexhaustible life of peace.

God declares anyone to be just who will justly trust him and take him at his Word in faith rather than endeavor to justify himself by trusting in his own merits (Psalm 143:2). As we trust and obey God through his divine Word Yeshua, the Father confers on us a new forgiven, accepted, righteous status before him as his sons. God in Yeshua has offered us acquittal, and if we obediently cling to Yeshua we **are** acquitted. Our transformation occurs as we grow to have the same mind towards sin as Yeshua does.

Yeshua comes to us and we are united to him not only in the mikveh-bris, not only in the Lord's Seder, but even in death when he will receive us as he did Stephen, the first Jewish martyr of the world-wide fellowship of the Jewish New Covenant (Acts 7:55, 59). We know that Yeshua will receive us then because we have received him now, and enjoy his Spirit already as an actual down-payment on our guaranteed eternal inheritance (Ephesians 1:14).

The Passover Seder of the Old Covenant looked backward to God's blood-sprinkled deliverance of his people from enslavement. This same festival also looked forward to the coming of the Messiah. The Passover Seder of the New Covenant also looks backward to a blood-sprinkled deliverance effected by the Lamb of God. This New Covenant Seder, however, looks forward to the Second Coming of the Messiah.

THE IMPORTANCE OF THE LORD'S SEDER SERVICE

Just as the mikveh-bris is an acted confession of our faith-union with Messiah, so is the Lord's Seder. On the last Sunday of the month (Acts 2:42 Sunday), when we stand from our seats to partake of the Lord's Seder, those who have not yet submitted to the mikveh-bris, are instructed to remain seated in order that they may witness our visible confession. When the server steps in front of each one of us with the broken matzoh of the Lord's body and the wine of his out-poured life, we are confronted with the very One who alone can free us and give us new life of peace, Yeshua Ha Mashiach. As the server says to us, "For every time you eat this bread and drink this cup, you proclaim the death of the Lord until he comes," we realize that as we concretely receive the saving Word of God, who is the Lamb of God who takes away the sin of the world, our very eating and drinking becomes preaching as we witness to the wonderful fact that we have been "passed over" and our sins have been forgiven so that we could have new life. As servers move around the room, the words, "For every time you eat this bread and drink this cup . . . " reverberate over and over again, even as the Gospel is echoing endlessly right now all over the world. This is a corporate sermon, preached by both the servers and the served, and does not end until the Messianic rabbi is himself served. When the last server has come forward and has served the Messianic rabbi, what a moment of intense worship ensues! For now we have just received the most precious Person in the world afresh and by the power of the Holy Spirit he indwells us all, with his presence most acutely experienced at this very moment. With our hands in the air we worship and adore the God of Israel and his Messiah. Praise God! Baruch Ha Shem! With overflowing love our hands reach out to one another as we experience our unity in him and affirm our love for one another by our touching.

The eternal Torah of God, the Word that was with God and was God from the beginning, has written himself afresh on our hearts! The perfect High Priest without beginning or end is in our midst! Hallelujah! He has made us One people!

Now, we see how important it is for us to obey the Lord's command that we celebrate the Lord's Supper, which is not an option but a divinely-imposed duty (see I Corinthians 11:24-25). The Lord Yeshua commands that we "do this," and that when we do, we are preaching the saving significance of the Lord's death, which is the Good News of Messianic Judaism (I Corinthians 11:26). Therefore, as spiritual Jews, it is our sacred duty to make every effort to attend Acts 2:42 Sunday so that we may "persistently" (Acts 2:42) preach in this divinely ordained manner and thus have the joy of sharing with others our salvation in the Lord.

As we conclude the Lord's Seder service each believer should be in prayer for the unbaptized who sat observing the corporate sermon Yeshua has just preached through us. We should pray that each one here today will stop excluding himself from our Lord's Seder, but will instead obey Yeshua and submit to the mikveh-bris so that, as a spiritual Jew, he will be no more excluded from this Passover table.

See Galatians 3:10-14; Romans 8:15-16; I Corinthians 6:19-20; Isaiah 53:10-12; I Peter 1:18-19; Hebrews 9:2-11; Ephesians 1:7; Romans 3:23-24; Mark 10:45.

A Lord's Seder Service

The Reader, standing:	In the same way that the story of the exodus from Egypt is retold and relived perpetually among the Jews on Passover, we who are spiritual Jews are commanded to retell and relive what happened for us on Passover in the death of our Lord Yeshua, who commands us, in our own Haggadah or "declaration," "Do this in remembrance of me."
	The Servers will come take their positions at the Lord's table beside the Reader.
The Reader:	Maranatha.
The Servers:	Our Lord, come.
The Reader:	Even so, come, Lord Yeshua.
The Servers:	Come.
The Reader:	Rabbi Saul, standing at the foot of a New Sinai, wrote this Haggadah for a new pilgrim spiritual Israel. The Lord's Supper is the Passover Seder of the Jewish New Covenant. Believers' Passover celebrates the New Exodus from the bondage of sin and death which the Jewish Messiah effected by his atoning death. Messiah Yeshua replaced the victim of the Old Covenant, the Passover lamb sacrificed in the festival of deliverance, and his blood ratified the New Covenant between God and man. The Jewish New Covenant (Jeremiah 31:31-34) promised forgiveness of sins and personal knowledge of and communion with God. By having followed the Lord through the Red Sea

of water immersion we have entered into
personal communion with God and, having
become spiritual Jews, may now come to the
Lord's Seder, even as we will someday feast at
the glorious Messianic banquet in the New
Jerusalem. This broken loaf and this out-
poured wine proclaim to all the Lord's death,
as well as the present time of salvation and the
coming judgment of the One who commanded
that we witness to him in this way: the King
of Israel, praised be he, Yeshua Ha Mashiach.

The Reader: v'lo ah-cha-ched mee-cam eh-chye ah-sher ah-vo-
tey-nu ha-yoo choo-lam tah-chat heh-ah-nahn
v'choo-lam ahv-roo b'toch ha-yahm.v'choo-lam
neet-b'loo l'mo-sheh beh-ah-nahn oo-v'yahm[1]

"You should understand, my brothers, that
our ancestors were all under the pillar of
cloud, and all of them passed through the Red
Sea; and so they all received immersion into
the fellowship of Moses in cloud and sea."[1]

v'zeh hoo oht ha-t'vee-lah ah-sher cah-et to-shee-
ah gahm oh-tah-nu lo v'hah-seer tee-noof hah-
bah-sahr kee eem bee-shahl lah-noo may-et eh-
lo-heem roo-ach sh'lay-mah ahl y'day hah-kah-
maht yeshua ha-mah-shee-ach[2]

"This water prefigured the water of baptism
through which you are now delivered to safety.
Baptism is not the washing away of bodily
uncleanness, but the appeal made to God by a
clear conscience; and it brings salvation
through the resurrection of Yeshua Ha
Mashiach."[2]

[1] I Corinthians 10:1-2 (NEB)

[2] I Peter 3:21

60

The Reader:

וְלֹא אֶחָד מִכֶּם אָחִי אֲשֶׁר אֲבוֹתֵינוּ
הָיוּ כֻלָם תַּחַת הֶעָנָן וְכֻלָם עָבְרוּ בְּתוֹךְ
הַיָם: וְכֻלָם נִטְבְּלוּ לְמשֶׁה בֶּעָנָן וּבַיָם:

וְזֶה הוּא אוֹת הַטְבִילָה אֲשֶׁר כָּעֵת תּוֹשִׁיעַ
גַּם־אֹתָנוּ לֹא בְהָסִיר טִנּוּף הַבָּשָׂר כִּי
אִם־בִּשְׁאָל־לָנוּ מֵאֵת אֱלֹהִים רוּחַ שְׁלֵמָה
עַל־יְדֵי הֲקָמַת יֵשׁוּעַ הַמָּשִׁיחַ:

The Reader:
(continued)

v'choo-lahm ahch-loo mah-ah-chol eh-chad roo-cha-nee. v'choo-lahm shah-too mahsh-keh eh-chad roo-cha-nee kee shah-too meen ha-tsoor ha-roo-chah-nee ha-ho-lech eemah-hem v'ha-tsoor hah-hoo hah-yah ha-mah-shee-ach. ah-vahl b'roo-bahm lo rah-tsah hah-elo-heem oo-feeg-ray-hem nahf-loo vah-meed-bar. v'chol zoht hah-y'tah lah-noo l'moh-fet l'veel-tee heet-ah-voht l'rah-ah cah-ah-sher heet-ah-voo gahm hey-mah[3]

"They all ate the same supernatural food, and all drank the same supernatural drink; I mean, they all drank from the supernatural rock that accompanied their travels — and that rock was Messiah. And yet, most of them were not accepted by God, for the desert was strewn with their corpses. These events happened as symbols to warn us not to set our desires on evil things, as they did."[3]

Therefore, we are to take no part in the Lord's Seder without applying moral scrutiny to our lives and behavior.

The Reader:

lah-cheyn mee sheh-yoh-chahl meen hah-lechem hah-zeh oh yeesh-teh mee-cohs hah-ah-dohn sheh-loh chah-rah-oo yeh-shahm l'goof ah-doh-ney-noo oo-l'dah-moh. yeev-chahn ha-eesh et nahf-sho v'ahz yoh-chal meen hah-lechem v'yeesh-teh meen hah-cohs. kee hah-oh-chel v'hah-sho-teh sheh-lo cha-rah-oo oh-chel v'shoh-teh deen l'naf-sho yah-ahn ah-sher lo heef-lah et-goof hah-ah-dohn[4]

"It follows that anyone who eats the bread or drinks the cup of the Lord unworthily will be guilty of desecrating the body and blood of the Lord. A man must examine himself before eating his share of the bread and drinking from the cup. For he who eats and drinks eats and drinks judgment on himself if he does not discern the Body."[4]

[3]I Corinthians 10:3-6   (NEB)

[4]I Corinthians 11:27-29   (NEB)

The Reader:

וְכֻלָם אָכְלוּ מַאֲכָל אֶחָד רוּחָנִי: וְכֻלָם
שָׁתוּ מַשְׁקֶה אֶחָד רוּחָנִי כִּי שָׁתוּ מִן־הַצּוּר
הָרוּחָנִי הַהֹלֵךְ עִמָּהֶם וְהַצּוּר הַהוּא הָיָה
הַמָּשִׁיחַ: אֲבָל בְּרֻבָּם לֹא רָצָה הָאֱלֹהִים
וּפִגְרֵיהֶם נָפְלוּ בַּמִּדְבָּר: וְכָל־זֹאת
הָיְתָה־לָּנוּ לְמוֹפֵת לְבִלְתִּי הִתְאַוֹּת לְרָעָה
כַּאֲשֶׁר הִתְאַוּוּ גַּם־הֵמָּה:

The Reader:

לָכֵן מִי שֶׁיֹּאכַל מִן־הַלֶּחֶם הַזֶּה אוֹ־יִשְׁתֶּה
מִכּוֹס   הָאָדוֹן שֶׁלֹּא כָרָאוּי יֶאְשַׁם   לְגוּף
אֲדֹנֵינוּ וּלְדָמוֹ: יִבְחַן הָאִישׁ אֶת־נַפְשׁוֹ וְאָז
יֹאכַל מִן־הַלֶּחֶם וְיִשְׁתֶּה   מִן־הַכּוֹס: כִּי
הָאֹכֵל   וְהַשֹּׁתֶה שֶׁלֹּא כָרָאוּי אֹכֵל וְשֹׁתֶה
דִין לְנַפְשׁוֹ יַעַן אֲשֶׁר לֹא־הִפְלָה אֶת־גּוּף
הָאָדוֹן:

(Those who have not yet obeyed the Lord by taking the mikveh-bris of water immersion in his name, please remain seated. This is to protect anyone from partaking unworthily in disobedience and bringing judgment upon himself. Those who have followed the Lord in the mikveh-bris of water immersion, please stand.)

The Reader: hah-lo yeh-dah-tem kee m'aht s'ohr m'chah-metz et kol hah-ee-sah. bah-ah-roo et hah-s'ohr hah-yah-shahn l'mah-ahn tee-yoo ee-sah chah-dah-shah hah-lo lechem matzot ah-tem kee gahm lah-noo fees-chey-noo hah-neez-bach bah-ah-deh-noo hoo ha-mah-shee-ach. seh ha-elo-heem ha-noh-seh cha-taht ha-oh-lahm[5]

"Have you never heard the saying, 'A little leaven leavens all the dough'? The old leaven of corruption is working among you. Purge it out, and then you will be bread of a new baking. As believers you are unleavened Passover bread; for indeed our Passover has begun; the sacrifice is offered — Messiah himself, the Lamb of God who takes away the sin of the world."[5]

(During the next few moments there will be silence as each believer shall conduct a mental search through every corner of his life to purge out in confession all the leaven of sin in order that he may be pronounced 'clean' by our God.)

The People, standing: ah-doh-nai neet-vah-deh et chah-toh-tey-noo

Lord, we confess our sins.

[5] I Corinthians 5:6-7; John 1:29 (NEB)

The Reader:

הֲלֹא יְדַעְתֶּם כִּי מְעַט שְׂאֹר מְחַמֵּץ
אֶת־כָּל־הָעִסָּה: בַּעֲרוּ אֶת־הַשְּׂאוֹר הַיָּשָׁן
לְמַעַן תִּהְיוּ עִסָּה חֲדָשָׁה הֲלֹא לֶחֶם מַצּוֹת
אַתֶּם כִּי גַם־לָנוּ פִּסְחֵנוּ הַנִּזְבָּח בַּעֲדֵנוּ הוּא
הַמָּשִׁיחַ: שֵׂה הָאֱלֹהִים הַנֹּשֵׂא חַטַּאת
הָעוֹלָם:

The People,
standing:

אֲדֹנָי נִתְוַדֶּה אֶת־חַטֹּאתֵינוּ

65

The Reader: v'eem neet-vah-deh et cha-toh-tay-noo neh-eh-
mahn hoo v'tsah-deek lees-loh-ach lah-noo et
cha-toh-tay-noo ool-tah-h'ray-noo me-kol ah-
vohn. nees-l'choo lah-chem cha-toh-tay-chem
l'mah-ahn sh'moh[6]

"If we confess our sins, he is just, and may be
trusted to forgive our sins and cleanse us from
every kind of wrong. Your sins are forgiven
you for his name's sake."[6]

The People,   Just as the Old Covenant was inaugurated by
standing: blood sacrifice, so too is the New Covenant.
We who enter into covenant with the Lord
through his blood enter also into covenant
with our fellow believers. Hereby united in
love concretely in this covenant meal, we are
established in the community of Messiah. We
are Spiritual Israel. We belong to one another
forever and to the Lord.

v'sheef-too ah-tehm et ah-sher oh-meyr. cohs
ha-b'rah-cha ah-sher ah-nach-noo m'vah-rech-
eem ha-loh hee heet-cha-b'root dahm ha-mah-
shee-ach v'ha-lechem ah-sher ah-nach-noo voh-
tseem ha-loh hoo heet-cha-b'root goof ha-mah-
shee-ach. kee lechem eh-chad hoo lah-chen-
gahm goof eh-chad ah-nach-noo ha-rah-beem
bah-ah-sher l'choo-lah-noo che-lak bah-lechem
hah-echod[7]

"Form your own judgment on what I say.
When we bless the cup of blessing, is it not a
means of sharing in the blood of Messiah?
When we break the bread, is it not a means of
sharing in the body of Messiah? Because there
is one loaf, we, many as we are, are one body,
for it is one loaf of which we all partake."[7]

The Reader,   ba-ruch atah adonai elohenu meh-lech ha'olam,
holding up   hamotzi lechem min ha-ah-retz.
the matzoh: Blessed art thou, O Lord our God, King of
the universe, who brings forth bread from the
earth.

[6] I John 1:9; I John 2:12 (NEB)

[7] I Corinthians 10:15-17 (NEB)

The Reader:

וְאִם־נִתְוַדֶּה אֶת־חַטֹּאתֵינוּ נֶאֱמָן הוּא וְצַדִּיק

לִסְלֹחַ   לָנוּ   אֶת־חַטֹּאתֵינוּ   וּלְטַהֲרֵנוּ

מִכָּל־עָוֹן: נִסְלְחוּ לָכֶם חַטֹּאתֵיכֶם לְמַעַן

שְׁמוֹ:

The People:

וּשְׁפַטְתוּ אַתֶּם אֶת אֲשֶׁר אָמַר: כּוֹס הַבְּרָכָה

אֲשֶׁר   אֲנַחְנוּ   מְבָרְכִים   הֲלֹא   הִיא

הִתְחַבְּרוּת   דַּם   הַמָּשִׁיחַ   וְהַלֶּחֶם   אֲשֶׁר

אֲנַחְנוּ   בֹּצְעִים   הֲלֹא   הוּא   הִתְחַבְּרוּת   גּוּף

הַמָּשִׁיחַ: כִּי־לֶחֶם   אֶחָד   הוּא   לָכֵן   גַּם־גּוּף

אֶחָד   אֲנַחְנוּ   הָרַבִּים   בַּאֲשֶׁר   לְכֻלָּנוּ   חֵלֶק

בַּלֶּחֶם   הָאֶחָד:

The Reader,   holding up the matzoh:

בָּרוּךְ   אַתָּה   יְיָ,   אֱלֹהֵינוּ   מֶלֶךְ   הָעוֹלָם,   הַמּוֹצִיא

לֶחֶם   מִן   הָאָרֶץ.

67

The Reader: kee cho kee-bahl-tee ah-noh-chee meen hah-ah-
(continued)   dohn et ah-sher gahm mah-sahr-tee lah-chem
                       kee hah-ah-dohn yeshua bah-lye-lah hah-hoo ah-
                       sher neem-sar boh lah-kach et hah-lechem. vah-
                       y'vah-rech vah-yeev-tsah vah-yoh-mer k'choo
                       eech-loo zeh goofee hah-neev-tsah bah-ahd-chem
                       ah-soo zoht l'zeech-roh-nee[8]

"For the tradition which I handed on to you came to me from the Lord himself: that the Lord Yeshua, on the night of his arrest, took bread and, after giving thanks to God, broke it and said: 'This is my body, which is for you; do this as a memorial of me.'"[8]

(Reader breaks matzoh)

The Reader,   ba-ruch atah adonai elohenu meh-lech ha'olam,
holding up   bo-reh p'ree hagafen.
the wine   Blessed art thou, O Lord our God, King of
and the cup: the universe, who creates the fruit of the vine.

          v'chen gahm et hah-cohs ah-char hah-s'oo-dah
          vah-yoh-mahr hah-cohs hah-zoht hee hah-b'reet
          ha-cha-dah-shah b'dah-mee ah-soo zoht l'zeech-
          ro-nee b'chol et sheh-teesh-too[9]

"In the same way, he took the cup after supper and said: 'This is the New Covenant sealed by my blood. Whenever you drink it, do this as a memorial of me.'"[9]

(Reader pours wine)

          kee b'chol et sheh-tohch-loo et ha-lechem ha-
          zeh v'teesh-too et hah-cohs ha-zoht hahz-ker
          tahz-kee-roo et moht ah-doh-ney-noo ahd kee
          yah-voh[10]

"For every time you eat this bread and drink the cup, you proclaim the death of the Lord, until he comes."[10]

(After the servers are served by the reader, they use the same formula [I Corinthians 11:26] to serve all who are standing, until they return to the table, where one of them serves the reader.)

The Reader: Let us raise our hands and worship the Lord.
                Maranatha.

[8] I Corinthians 11:23-24 (NEB)

[9] I Corinthians 11:25 (NEB)

[10] I Corinthians 11:26 (NEB)

The Reader:

כִּי־כֹה קִבַּלְתִּי אָנֹכִי מִן־הָאָדוֹן אֶת־אֲשֶׁר
גַּם־מָסַרְתִּי לָכֶם כִּי הָאָדוֹן יֵשׁוּעַ בַּלַּיְלָה
הַהוּא אֲשֶׁר־נִמְסַר בּוֹ לָקַח אֶת־הַלֶּחֶם:
וַיְבָרֶךְ וַיִּבְצַע וַיֹּאמַר קְחוּ אִכְלוּ זֶה גוּפִי
הַנִּבְצָע בַּעַדְכֶם עֲשׂוּ־זֹאת לְזִכְרוֹנִי:

(Reader breaks matzoh)
The Reader, *holding up the wine and the cup:*

בָּרוּךְ אַתָּה יְיָ, אֱלֹהֵינוּ מֶלֶךְ הָעוֹלָם, בּוֹרֵא
פְּרִי הַגָּפֶן.

וְכֵן גַּם־ אֶת־הַכּוֹס אַחַר הַסְּעוּדָה וַיֹּאמַר
הַכּוֹס הַזֹּאת הִיא הַבְּרִית הַחֲדָשָׁה בְּדָמִי
עֲשׂוּ־זֹאת לְזִכְרוֹנִי בְּכָל־עֵת שֶׁתִּשְׁתּוּ:

(Reader pours wine)

כִּי בְכָל־עֵת שֶׁתֹּאכְלוּ אֶת־הַלֶּחֶם הַזֶּה
וְתִשְׁתּוּ אֶת־הַכּוֹס הַזֹּאת הַזֵּכֶר תַּזְכִּירוּ
אֶת־מוֹת אֲדֹנֵינוּ עַד כִּי יָבוֹא:

The Prayer Life of a Spiritual Jew

Here is the most important prayer you'll ever have the opportunity to pray. Take a moment to meditate on the thoughts it conveys. Then make these words your own as you speak them to God in faith.

God of Abraham, Isaac and Jacob: I am a Jew and I'm going to die a Jew. But I've decided to stop living as I please. I promise to live by your Word as it's recorded in the entire Bible, including the New Testament. Father, I know that you can justly forgive my sins only through the punishment of Yeshua. Yeshua, I believe that you overcame death to prove that you are part of God, my Messiah and my Lord. Come into my life. Forgive my sins. Take control of my life through your Holy Spirit. And I'll obey you forever. Thank you, Father. In Yeshua's name I pray. Amen.

WHAT IS PRAYER?

Many of us pray only about once a year, treating God like a kind of Jewish Santa Claus — useful in a pinch, when we send up our "request lists" to him. But actually we'd rather be "adult" and never have to "sit on his lap." "God helps them that help themselves," we say. "Besides, what good does it do?" We can all remember at least one thing we whispered into his ear that we didn't get. Having said that, we rationalize ourselves back into our father Adam's mistake: like him we try to make it through life on our own. Our lack of prayer shows the degree of our sinful independence from God and scant trust in him.

Our Lord Yeshua taught that we should not take his Father for granted, as though he were a mere suggestion box to use

70

and then forget about. Rather, when we pray, we should pray with great depth of fervor and persistence, basing all our hope in the Father's generosity (Matthew 7:7-11), yet praying with great intensity (Mark 13:33, 14:38; Matthew 26:41) and burden of heart.

Prayer is no mere grocery listing of every man's personal wishes. Prayer is our most intimate and beautiful experience with God, ranging through the ultimate capacities of human feelings, from ecstatic thanksgiving to serene communion.

Many of us say we're too busy with charity and other endeavors to pray. We forget that good works are no substitute for prayer, even though loving acts should be the outgrowth of loving thoughts. But prayer is more than thinking! Prayer is working, too. **Prayer changes things!** That is, if prayers are addressed to the One who is responsive to all prayer uttered in the name of his Son, **then** prayer changes things. Only this One is the God of Israel.

And the amazing fact about this wonderful God of ours is that he has the generosity to share with us his power! He does this by allowing us to be co-workers with him not only in what we do but also in what we pray. Yeshua's prayers changed the world. He was not merely retreating for a rest when he prayed alone in the wilderness. By releasing the power of his Father through prayers said secretly in the night, he would be able to demonstrate that same power openly in the miracles he performed in the day. Our prayers can have the same power.

Prayer is not an experiment. Prayer is seizing from the Word of God by the hand of faith the will of God **for this moment**: confessing the sins enumerating by God's Word, praising and adoring the God revealed by his Word, claiming the promises of God's Word.

Prayer is engaging in spiritual warfare, coming against cosmic powers of darkness to banish them by the mighty name of Yeshua. Prayer is binding the evil one and releasing what belongs to God and God's people, whether it be finances or food or property or whatever. Our weapon is divinely potent to demolish demonic strongholds (II Corinthians 10:4). Our weapon is the armor of prayer (Ephesians 6:13-20).

Yeshua Ha Mashiach has bound the Devil, and as members of his Body, we can share in his victory. By exerting Yeshua's authority we can bind Satan and "spoil his house." All we need is enough faith to throw ourselves into prayer with a victory shout for Yeshua on our lips as we claim all he has

made possible for us to claim in his Name: sustenance, healings, deliverance, miracles, everything. The only thing that can
stop us is our lack of faith (Matthew 17:20, 21). The only
things that can hinder us are weak, tentative, rambling prayers,
where we allow Satan to convince us we're not being heard or
our prayers don't really affect the heart of God or retard the
power of the Devil.

Our prayers must be uttered in faith, believing all things
are possible. When we pray, our Lord Yeshua asks us the same
question he asked the blind men in Matthew 9:28: "Do you
believe that I am able to do this?" If we ask the Father anything in the Son's Name, then we imply that we do believe
Yeshua is able, not only to hear our prayers but to make
known the Father to us and keep us in the Father's will.

Messiah Yeshua asks us to heal the sick, to bind the
demonic, to proclaim good news to every creature. How can
we rise to such heights unless we are, like him, men of
prayer? We too must be swept along by the power of his
resurrection, which is the power of the Holy Spirit who
inspires us in our prayers.

TO WHOM DO WE PRAY?

"Our Father in heaven" is not meant to conjure up an old
man with a white beard, but a loving, life-giving personal
creator. Therefore we pray to the "Father of mercy" — a
term still found in the Prayer Book.

We **know** God hears our prayers because we **know** we are
his sons and he is our Father. How do we know he is our
Father? We know he is our Father because we accepted him
as our Father when we accepted his Son as our Messiah and
Lord.

Everyone who believes that Yeshua is the Messiah is a child
of God (I John 5:1).

To prove that we are sons, God has sent into our hearts
the spirit of his Son, crying "Abba! Father!" We are therefore
no longer slaves but sons, and if sons, then also, by God's
own act, heirs (Galatians 4:6-7).

"Abba" is the most affectionate and intimate term of
endearment that a Jewish child has in his vocabulary for his
father. There is no example of God ever being referred to as
Abba in Judaism before Yeshua appeared in Israel. No one
had ever known the God of Israel that intimately before

72

Yeshua. But Yeshua had always been with his Father, even before he came among us as a man. In fact Yeshua was part of the Father's very being: his glorious life-creating Word whom the Father loved as his only Son. This One came from the Father to reveal the Father so that men might know the Father as Abba.

The Father gives to men on the basis of his love for his Son and because of his Son's righteous sacrifice. Yeshua instructed the first Jewish believers to begin making their requests to the Father in the name of his Son, for whose sake only the Father can rightly bless sinners such as themselves.

But to whom do we pray, the Father or the Son? There is prayer to the Lord Yeshua in the Jewish New Covenant Scriptures (see Revelation 22:20), so it cannot be considered unjewish to address prayer to him. Two of the greatest Jews who ever lived did precisely that. (See Acts 7:59 and II Corinthians 12:8 where Stephen and Rabbi Saul pray to Yeshua.) From the very first, Jewish believers hailed Yeshua as One worthy of worship and adoration and prayer.

Prayers of adoration and praise are very properly addressed to our Lord Yeshua, who loved us enough to die for us in order that his Father could forgive us.

"To deny honor to the Son is to deny honor to the Father who sent him" (John 5:23). However, our Lord Yeshua himself taught us to direct our petitions toward his Father in Yeshua's name. For it is in Yeshua's name that the Father is revealed and is actively present to men.

Yeshua taught, "No one knows the Father except the Son and any one to whom the Son chooses to reveal him" (Matthew 11:27). "In very truth I tell you, if you ask the Father for anything in my name, he will give it to you. So far you have asked nothing in my name. Ask and you will receive, that your joy may be complete" (John 16:23-24).

A distinctively Jewish conception of God is that he is "our Father," a merciful Father to those who are his obedient sons. However, this great God had always seemed so awesome that the Jewish people had not been comfortable referring to God as "our Father" before the Son came to reveal the Father. But the Father was brought near to men through the Son, and because of our knowledge of the Son, we can pray to the Father in the Son's name with a new intimacy toward God based on a new and personal knowledge of him.

Yeshua gave Judaism a new prayer. Whereas before his

coming, Judaism could address God with only the ceremonial formality appropriate to a monarch, with the appearance of God's Son who invites all men to experience divine sonship, a new style and spirit of prayer is possible. Thus Jesus could pray not only the set prayers in Hebrew, he prayed in his mother-tongue (Aramaic) and taught his disciples to pray like him, even giving them a set prayer in their mother-tongue, Aramaic, which came to be called the Lord's Prayer.

"Our Father who is in heaven" (see Matthew 6:9-13 and Luke 11:2-4), is a Jewish prayer that teaches the proper sense of dependence on God for all human needs, from the loftiest aspiration (a world where God's Name is revered) to the most ordinary request (food). This sense of dependence is cultivated by table grace such as practiced by our Lord Yeshua, who not only blessed his Father before a meal but also offered thanks afterward. Frequent prayer instills a truly realistic attitude to life, since God is the universal giver of life and breath, and it is only in him that we live and move and have our being. To habitually fail to acknowledge our dependence and gratitude to God is to lose touch with reality and with the source of life itself. Prayer is as vital as breathing to our spiritual well-being. Just as the devout Jew prays for God's protection and blessing at midday and before retiring, so also he prays as soon as he opens his eyes in the morning, so immediate is his awareness of his need for God.

Abba is a holy word for our Father in heaven. We are not to use this title when we address any man (Matthew 23:9). We can refer to the God of the universe in this intimately familiar way because we are members of his family. Children can call their father "Abba" (see Romans 8:15 and Galatians 4:6).

WHAT ARE WE TO PRAY FOR?

Our Father
Abba, revered be thy name
Thy kingdom come
Thy will be done
On earth as it is in heaven
Tomorrow's bread, give us today
And forgive us, as we have forgiven others.
Do not let us be carried away by temptation
Keep us from joining the Evil One
For thine is the kingdom and the power and the glory forever, Amen.

In the Lord's Prayer, our Lord Yeshua prayed for his Father — for his name, his kingdom, and his will — and he prayed for himself and his fellow men — for bread, forgiveness, and victory over evil. This is a model prayer for any believer.

Yeshua commands us to pray for our enemies: "Bless them that curse you, do good to them that hate you, and pray for them which despitefully use you and persecute you, that you may be children of your Father which is in heaven: for he makes his sun to rise on the evil and on the good, and sendeth rain on the just and unjust (see Matthew 5:44-45 and Leviticus 19:17-18).

Lord Yeshua teaches us to pray for our daily bread (Matthew 6:11), for forgiveness of those we wrong just as we forgive those who wrong us (Matthew 6:13), for laborers in the harvest field of Messianic Judaism's Gospel ministry (Matthew 9:38), for the sick (James 5:13-18), for wisdom (James 1:5), and for the Holy Spirit (Luke 11:13).

Rabbi Saul desired that spiritual Jews pray for knowledge (Philippians 1:9) and power issuing in the love of the Messiah Yeshua, through whom both as individuals and as brothers they should grow to maturity. He knew that it was only as spiritual Jews that they could pray effectively, for prayer is a gift of the Holy Spirit (see I Corinthians 14:14-16). In fact, the believer prays "in the Spirit."

We should pray for our government, because it is by means of human government that God holds the Devil's children in check. In fact, praying for human government should be the first order of business for believers, but it is only as human government acts on God's behalf to punish evil that the people of God can live in peace. (See II Thessalonians 2:5-8 where Rabbi Saul sees that it is only the restraining hand of government that keeps Anti-Christ from being revealed.) When human government crumbles, Anti-Christ will take advantage of the situation by amassing the world's population into a demonic anti-God super-society where no believer living at that time will be free of danger. Therefore, it is obvious why we should pray for our government.

Why is prayer so important? Because temptation is always terribly dangerous and near at hand. Selling out is the easiest thing in the world to do, and can be so cleverly rationalized that the deed is done before we feel the guilt pangs. Therefore we must pray — whether we feel like it or not, for when we least feel like praying, temptation is beckoning all the more seductively.

God gives us people to pray for and he gives us the privilege of influencing his dealings with those people. When an old friend comes to mind repeatedly or some person's face persists in our mind, this may be an invitation by God to hold that person up in prayer, for God is concerned that we be concerned for our fellow men.

If we wonder why our synagogue is not growing, if we wonder why our people are not confessing Yeshua as Lord in the mikveh, then we should examine the prayer life of our synagogue. Are we burdened to see people take the mikveh? Does it matter enough to us to agree on it in prayer? Are we praying daily for our Torah studies and teachers? Are we praying for the lost? Are we claiming victories in prayer?

If our people have no on-going prayer burden for the Jewish community near our sheul, our sheul will make no impact on our community. Since God takes us seriously as his co-workers, he takes our initiative seriously as well. If our prayer initiative is at a low ebb so will be the success of our prayer labor with the Lord. Our success hinges upon our expectant prayers and God's Spirit (see Philippians 1:19 and Ephesians 6:18-20).

When unbelievers refuse to come to believers' meetings, one of the most effective means of soul-winning is to establish a prayer-bond with them, informing them of our corporate prayers on behalf of their needs. The answers to prayer and the love displayed by prayer itself will be a sign to the unbeliever. He won't be able to help feeling somewhat obligated to the body of believers for praying for him. Our inexplicable love will draw him closer to attending believers' meetings, where the environment of faith will be a fertile seed bed for the unbeliever's faith to bud.

Finally, we should petition God for all our needs — physical, mental, spiritual, financial, whatever they are, whether for ourselves or for others — and praise him for being the generous and loving Father he is, to hear and answer our prayers. Praise him for every cheerful and good moment you enjoyed today and yesterday, for he prepared them all. Praise him, too, for the difficult times, for these will help us toughen toward endurance and maturity.

The shortened form of the Amidah from the prayer book is an excellent example of what to pray for:

"Give us wisdom, O Lord our God, to know thy ways: turn our will so that we will fear thee, and forgive us so that we may be saved. Keep us far from sadness; satisfy our needs from the food of thy land, and gather our scattered ones from the four corners of the earth. Let them that go astray be judged according to thy will, and bring thy hand upon the evil ones. Let the righteous rejoice in the rebuilding of thy city (Jerusalem), and in the establishment of thy temple, and in the flourishing of the power of David thy servant, and in the clear shining light of the son of Jesse, thy Messiah. Even before we call, do thou answer. Blessed art thou, O Lord, who hears prayer."

A list of the petitions in this prayer are 1) for divine wisdom, 2) divine help in the business of being obedient, 3) forgiveness, 4) freedom from sorrow, 5) physical sustenance, 6) unity for the people of God, 7) God's righteous punishment of the unrepentant wicked of the world, 8) the building up of Jerusalem, 9) the establishment of God's temple, and 10) the coming of the Davidic Messiah to bring order and holy light to a sin-darkened world.

However, we should remember that even the Talmud advises us that prayer must come from the heart, and not be the mere lip service paid to a fixed written prayer (see Pirke aboth II.18). No prayer should be read from a piece of paper unless it has been made one's own prayer by faith.

WHY PRAYERS MISS THEIR MARK

Prayer is power. Whatever power we have, however, is not from ourselves but from God's Spirit. "Not by might, not by power, but by my Spirit, saith the Lord." Therefore we must not presume to think that we can manipulate God into providing for our every whim. It is only as we have the mind of the Messiah that our will becomes God's will and we get whatever we ask for.

The Lord does not "hear" every prayer (see Isaiah 1:15; 29:13), but only the prayers of those who are coming into a covenantal relationship with him. To pray and be heard one must know the name of the Lord, the full name of the Lord: the Name of the Father and the Son and the Holy Spirit. Only then can one call on the Name of the Lord and be certain he is heard.

Therefore, one precondition of successful prayer is knowing who the Father is through a knowledge of his Son, for whose sake alone the Father is free to be gracious to sinners. For the Father can justly forgive sinners only because of the punishment of his Son, through whose death no sins went unpunished.

But knowing who God is isn't enough. One must also have faith (Mark 11:24). That is, one must believe that God is actually there and that he is free to act for the benefit of those who ask him (Hebrews 11:6). Other preconditions are: willingness to forgive others before presuming to ask for forgiveness (Matthew 6:14-15); making peace first (Matthew 5:23-24); humility (II Chronicles 7:14); whole-hearted intensity (Jeremiah 29:13); unwavering deliberation (James 1:6); righteous confession (I John 1:1-10; James 5:16); proper motives (James 4:3); the guidance of the Holy Spirit without whom no one would even know what to pray for (Romans 8:26-27); and especially a willingness to obey God's Word: "We can approach God with confidence, and obtain from him whatever we ask, because we are keeping his commands and doing whatever he approves" (I John 3:21-22). "If you dwell in me and my words dwell in you, you shall ask what you will and it shall be done unto you" (John 15:7).

If there is any area of your life where you are disobeying God, correct yourself immediately and ask God's forgiveness, or your disobedience will undermine your prayers. Have you taken the mikveh of Yeshua? You'd better do it, if you expect your prayers to be answered.

The Word of God lists other causes of failure in prayer: 1) self-indulgence (James 4:3), 2) stubbornness (Zechariah 7:13), 3) evil (Isaiah 59:2; Micah 3:4), 4) blood-guiltiness (Isaiah 1:15), 5) despising the law (Proverbs 28:9), 6) neglect of mercy (Proverbs 21:13), 7) indifference (Proverbs 1:28), 8) secret sin (Psalm 66:18), 9) disobedience (Deuteronomy 1:45; I Samuel 14:37; 28:6), and 10) sometimes prayer is refused because it is not in accord with the divine will (see II Corinthians 12:8-9).

When our Lord Yeshua made a request he always remained ready to bow to the will of his Father. Like him we must never let favorable answers to our prayers be a condition for our love toward God. However, many people use this principle as an excuse to pray in unbelief. "Lord, if it be thy will, heal this child," we hear believers pray. Often believers really don't have enough faith to claim a healing, so they use their uncertainty regarding the will of God to mask their uncertainty regarding God's power to heal. But the fact is that God has already revealed his will to us in his Word. Read what God says is his will regarding healing: "The prayer offered in faith will save the sick man, the Lord will raise him from his bed, and any sins he has committed will be forgiven. Therefore, confess your sins to one another, and pray for one another, and then you will be healed. A good man's prayer is powerful and effective" (James 5:15-16). *(NEB)*

We need to realize that our prayers **are** powerful if we have faith enough to claim all the promises of God's Word when we pray. For God keeps his Word and he sends his Spirit to honor his Word and to do all that his Word promises to do, including healing the sick. The Scripture says that God "sent his word and healed them and delivered them from their corruptions" (Psalm 107:20). Then in the fullness of time God sent his Word among us as a man who came to heal a lost and very sick world. This one who came was the Father's life-giving Word, that part of his being that was always with him and through whom he created everything. Thus Yeshua "went about doing good and healing all who were oppressed by the devil" (Acts 10:38).

Then the Son of God, who is the Word of God in person, promised his followers that he would send them the Holy Spirit from the Father (John 15:26) and that the Spirit would be their Helper in bearing witness to the Son through the miraculous acts they would perform in his name.

Referring to his acts (John 10:25), which elsewhere (John 9:3-4) include acts of healing, Yeshua declares, "In truth, in very truth I tell you, he who has faith in me will do what I am doing; and he will do greater things still because I am going to the Father. Indeed anything you ask in my name I will do, so that the Father may be glorified in the Son. If you ask anything in my name I will do it" (John 14:12-14).

Yeshua said, "The spirit alone gives life; the flesh is of no avail; the words which I have spoken to you are both spirit and life. And yet there are some of you who have no faith" (John 6:63-64).

Ephesians 3:20 says that Yeshua is able to do far more abundantly than all that we ask or think and he does it "by the power at work within us." There are indeed vast resources of his power open to us who believe (Ephesians 1:19), and we have been given authority to loose and bind on earth with the confidence that we will be backed up in heaven (Matthew 18:18). Therefore, we need only agree on a thing that the Word of God promises, and by faith release the power of God in Yeshua's name, letting our hands become his hands and our lips his lips, confident that God will accomplish whatever we will as like-minded ambassadors of his Son. Therefore, when we pray for the sick, we can pray, "Father, I claim the authority you have given me to do what our Lord Yeshua did. In his name, Father I release the power to heal this person and thank you in faith for performing this miracle in order that the Father may be glorified in the Son. Amen."

But we should be careful not to put a time limit on God's answers to our prayers. We can claim victories in Yeshua's name, but we cannot claim that God's time-table will always be our own. However, this does not mean we should **hope** our prayers will be answered. Faith is not hope. Faith is a present claim on God's promises here and now, believing right now that he is hearing and is acting to make good his word, though the manifest, final results may come only in the process of time.

Also, when you pray, don't depend entirely on other people's faith. Trust God yourself. Remember you are a child of God. You have been renewed in the image of his Son. You don't have to beg. As a son you can gratefully trust your heavenly Father to give you all that he has promised in his Word. For God promises, "I watch over my word to perform it" (Jeremiah 1:12). And don't just admire the Word of God, act on it! Don't just pray for faith, do what the word of God says in faith: confess your sins, believe, receive, release power to bless, take authority to bind, speak peace, speak healing, and do all in Yeshua's name, standing in his place. Remember: you are captured by what you confess (Proverbs 6:2). "Whoever has no inward doubts but believes that what he says is happening, it will be done for him" (Mark 11:23). "You do not get what you want because you do not pray for it" (James 4:2).

WHAT TO DO WHEN YOU PRAY

Prayer is talking with God. Therefore, Yeshua taught that our prayers are to be privately sincere rather than publicly showy, and reverently brief rather than heathenishly verbose

(Gentiles thought God was impressed by endless addresses). He says, "When you pray, go into a room by yourself, shut the door, and pray to your Father who is there in the secret place; and your Father who sees what is secret will reward you openly" (Matthew 6:6).

There is no place for self-conscious artifice or long-winded pomposity. Some people say, "I don't know how to pray," as though prayer were an unapproachably virtuous act. But Yeshua taught that speaking to one's Heavenly Father is as uncomplicated as communicating with one's earthly father, and infinitely more profitable (see Matthew 7:7-11) if persistent (see Luke 11:5-8 and 18:1-5).

Many people find that they can concentrate better on what they are saying to God if they pray aloud. Often silent prayers get distracted by other silent thoughts, and what began as a prayer time lapses into a ten minute daydream. For most people, then, audible prayer — even if it's only a whisper — is preferable to purely silent prayer, especially in one's daily devotions.

Almost any posture is Biblically permissible: 1) bowing (Exodus 4:31), 2) kneeling (Daniel 6:10), 3) on the face before God (Numbers 20:6), 4) standing (I Kings 8:22), 5) while dancing (Psalm 149:3) like David (II Samuel 6:14) and the modern Hasidim, 6) or while dovening (swaying forward and backward), 7) or lifting up the hands (Psalm 141:2).

Prayer should begin with the joyful acknowledgment that the most wonderful Person alive lives! We know he lives by the ordered creation he has given to us, by his Word, by the loving warmth of his Holy Spirit and by the invisible presence of his Risen Son, our Lord Yeshua. This knowledge is indeed joy unspeakable, to experience the presence of the very life of God, whose eternal life has been offered to us by his Son. No wonder we praise and adore the God of Israel! No wonder we must have time to worship and inhale his fragrant beauty before we intercede for others or make known our petitions.

The Scripture tells us that by Yeshua we are to "offer the sacrifice of praise to God continually, that is, the fruit of our lips giving thanks to his name" (Hebrews 13:15). This thought has been echoed in Rabbinic literature: "In the world to come, all sacrifice will cease, but the sacrifice of thanksgiving will remain forever; equally, all confessions will cease, but the confession of thanksgiving will remain forever" (Pesiqta de Rab Kahana 79a 17f).

The Scripture says, "Rejoice in the Lord always: and again I say rejoice (Philippians 4:4). Give thanks always for all things unto God and the Father in the name of our Lord Yeshua Ha Mashiach (Ephesians 5:20). "Whatever you do in word or deed do all in the name of the Lord Yeshua, giving thanks to God and the Father by him" (Colossians 3:17). "The Lord is near. Have no anxiety, but in everything by prayer and supplication with thanksgiving let your requests be made known unto God. Then the peace of God, which is beyond our utmost understanding, will keep guard over your hearts and your thoughts in Messiah Yeshua" (Philippians 4:6-7).

We should confess our sins to God daily and ask forgiveness in the name of Yeshua, for it is through his kaporrah that God can righteously overlook our wrongs. We should admit that we need God's help to overcome temptation. We should claim the Son's aid in helping us obey his Father, whose control of our life through the Holy Spirit will give us victory over all temptations and deliver us from the evil one. As we pray for mercy and grace, we have a great High Priest, both human and divine, interceding for us in heaven (Hebrews 4:14-16).

True prayer is responsiveness to the divine will so that each detail of our lives is open to molding and strengthening and help by God so that our lives will accomplish just precisely what God intended for them to accomplish. God wants us to pray about our personal problems and hang-ups (see Psalm 142). "Cast all your cares upon him because he cares about you" (I Peter 5:7). "In thy righteousness bring me out of trouble" (Psalm 143:11).

How do I know that God will help me now? Because he has acted in my behalf before. He acted for my people in three great events: at the exodus of Egypt, on the execution tree, and at the empty tomb.

One of the most effective ways to pray is to "put God in remembrance" (Isaiah 43:26) for some promise he has made in his word, and claim that promise in prayer, trusting God to keep his word. Speak out audibly like you mean what you say (Psalm 145:18-19) and afterwards patiently wait on the Lord (Psalm 27:14).

We know that Yeshua was brought up by devout Jewish parents and grew up learning the fixed prayers of his people in both his Nazareth home and synagogue. Few people notice his recitation of the Shema (Deuteronomy 6:4) in the Gospel of Mark (Mark 23:29), yet it is certain that Yeshua did not fail to observe the traditional three hours of prayer (morning, midday, and evening), and did not take a meal without first offering a blessing. When our Lord Yeshua prayed, he sought guidance (Luke 6:12), he interceded for others (John 17:6-26), and he communed with his Father (Luke 9:28). Yeshua interceded for a tempted disciple (Luke 22:31), for children (Mark 10:16), and for his people, the Jewish people (Matthew 23:37-39).

Prayer is not a merely private matter. It is also a privilege to be shared. When friends and neighbors intercede for one another with their Father, they build a love bond of strength between themselves and God. Their united prayer has power, too. Yeshua said, "If two of you agree on earth about any request you have to make, that request will be granted by my heavenly Father. For where two or three have met together in my name, I am there among them" (Matthew 18:19-20). Since our prayers have such power, we should plead for big as well as small causes, and not forget to pray for God's work and workers in the world, including ourselves. We should not only pray for the health of believers, but that God would **use** them according to his great purposes.

Corporate prayer is the Lord Yeshua's Body (two or more believers in him) agreeing together as it seeks the guidance and confirming strength of its Head and Lord. (On the importance of corporate prayers, read Hebrews 10:19-25.)

FASTING AS AN AID TO PRAYER

Our Lord Yeshua recommended fasting as an aid to prayer (Mark 9:29). Also see Matthew 9:15: "The day will come when the bridegroom is taken away from them . . . then they will fast." Our prayer life is often aided by fasting (that is, going without food for a time). Biblically considered, fasting may be abstaining from all foods (Acts 9:9) or from only certain foods (Daniel 10:3). Fasting may be a public endeavor, as on a fast day (Leviticus 23:27), or it may be private, unto the Lord (Zechariah 7:5) as an act of humility and repentance (Psalm 69:10) or positive dedication (Acts 13:3). Moreover, fasting is a means of seeking the Lord with all one's heart (Jeremiah 29:13-14; Ezra 8:23) or of changing God's mind (Jonah 3:5, 10). Fasting is also a means of sensitizing oneself to God for the purpose of spiritual warfare against satanic oppression (Isaiah 58:6) or demonic possession (Matthew 17: 21) or as a means of seeking God's face more sensitively for spiritual guidance or revelation (Daniel 9:2, 3, 21, 22).

DAILY FELLOWSHIP WITH YOUR FATHER

Can you imagine working with the most wonderful Father in the world? . . . Working intimately with him on the biggest and greatest projects possible in life? He is there through his Holy Spirit and his Word to direct your work as your prayer co-laborer (I Corinthians 3:9) as you step out with him in faith to execute every one of your prayer projects together. What victory celebrations you can have together! What love can pass between you!

Spend time with your Father in the morning. Take a message out of your Bible from him and savor the deep goodness of what he says. Let the possibilities of his promises loom up before you like the gates of heaven. Then thank your Father for everything you're going to need that day, taking deep satisfaction from the fact that he hears you. Prayer is communication to the Father, in the name of the Son, through the inspiration of the indwelling Holy Spirit and according to God's will as expressed in his Word. What better way to start the day?

Model prayers and key verses for study: I Thessalonians 3: 11-13; Colossians 1:9, 10; Psalm 6, 51, 103; I John 5:14, 15; Matthew 26:41-42; Hebrews 4:16; Jeremiah 33:3.

Messianic Synagogue Stewardship

Would you hide stolen money in your house? If someone had some "hot" money he'd like you to harbor, to hide under your bed or whatever, would you do it? No, you wouldn't. Well, suppose it was God's money? Would you try to harbor God's money? Of course you wouldn't, because you'd know that God is not fooled. You'd realize that you'd have to face him and explain to him why you'd held out on him and kept him from using his own money. If you cancel the use of God's money for his own plans, you're going to hear from God! You'd certainly know that **you** wouldn't like it if you had money and you had plans for it and people's lives were eternally at stake in the matter, and someone came along and denied you the use of your own money. God doesn't like it either. Read what he says:

> "Will a man rob God? Yet you have robbed me. But you say, how have we robbed thee? In tithes and offerings. You are cursed with a curse, the whole nation of you. Bring ye all the tithes into the storehouse that there may be meat in mine house, and prove me now herewith, says the Lord of Hosts, if I will not open you the windows of heaven, and pour you out a blessing, that there shall not be room enough to receive it" (Malachi 3:8-10).

THE OBVIOUS GONIFF

There are essentially three ways to rob God. The first way is the most obvious: **simply steal God's tithe outright.** This is the Obvious Goniff. The Obvious Goniff doesn't care about God's generosity, or about the fact that everything we receive is a gift from God, or that God loans us $10 but only asks that we return $1. The Obvious Goniff doesn't care.

The Obvious Goniff is like the man God loaned $2,000.

85

Then one day, God came to the man and said, "Listen, you can keep $1,800."

"Really?" the man exclaimed. "Praise the Lord, I don't have to give back the $1,800!"

"I just came by to pick up my $200," said God.

"**GET OFF MY BACK!**" the man said.

Many people are like this man. They don't want to hear anything about giving God money, when in effect he has really given **them** the money, and they are stealing **his** money if they refuse to return one-tenth of it to him. "The silver is mine and the gold is mine, says the Lord of Hosts" (Haggai 2:8). "Every good present and every perfect gift is from above, coming down from the Father of lights with whom there is no variation or shadow due to change" (James 1:17).

Obvious goniffs are guilty of the sin of covetousness which is idolatry and is, according to the Scriptures, the sure sign of a pagan or non-Jew (see Colossians 3:5). Yeshua taught us not to have heathenish anxieties about money but to set our enterprise on storing up rewards for ourselves in heaven rather than here on earth.

"Do not ask anxiously, 'What are we to eat? What are we to drink? What shall we wear?' All these are things for the heathen to run after, not for you, because your heavenly Father knows that you need them all. Concentrate on God's kingdom and his justice before everything else, and all the rest will come to you as well. So do not worry about tomorrow; tomorrow will worry about itself. Each day has troubles enough of its own" (Matthew 6:31-34).

Rabbi Saul echoes Yeshua's promise when he writes, "And my God will supply all your wants out of the magnificence of his riches in Messiah Yeshua" (Philippians 4:19). "Instruct those who are rich in this world's goods not to be uppish, and not to fix their hopes on so uncertain a thing as money, but upon God, who provides us richly with all things to enjoy. Tell them to do good and to grow rich in good deeds, to be ready to give away and to share, and so acquire a treasure which will form a good foundation for the future. Thus they will grasp the life which is life indeed" (I Timothy 6:17-19).

As far as each local body of believers is concerned, here is what Rabbi Saul wrote about weekly giving: "And now about the collection in aid of God's people: you should follow my instructions to our congregations in Galatia. Every Sunday each of you is to put aside and keep by him a sum in proportion to his gains" (I Corinthians 16:2).

But what proportion? The tithe has always been one tenth. In fact, that's what the word "tithe" means, one tenth. God demands from us only $1 back for every $10 he increases us, letting us keep $9. Just as in the synagogue every adult male was under obligation to contribute to the expenses of the Jerusalem Temple, in the same way spiritual Jews, whether they be physically male or female, Jew or Gentile, adult or child, are under obligation to set aside a proportion (10%) of that which God prospers them for the upbuilding of the Body of Yeshua in their local assembly. Also, each local assembly is to give at least 10% of its total tithes to world missions so that the Body of Yeshua around the world may advance.

There are those who say, "I can't live on $9 out of every $10 I receive. I've got to have all $10 to live, especially in times like these. But those who are materially tight with God will discover a certain spiritual and/or financial poverty in their own life. "He who sows sparingly will also reap sparingly, and he who sows bountifully will also reap bountifully" (II Corinthians 9:6). We should give "neither reluctantly nor under compulsion, for God loves a cheerful giver. And thus you may always have enough of everything and may provide in abundance for every good work" (II Corinthians 9:7-8). Therefore, like the Macedonian believers in II Corinthians 8:2, we can afford to give in faith even when we are suffering financial depression.

Moreover, when we become disciples of Yeshua we must count the cost. If we're not willing to sacrifice our lives, Yeshua tells us that we cannot be his disciples. And if we're not willing to make any kind of financial sacrifice, we're only kidding ourselves saying we want to be disciples of Yeshua. If we can't face the offering plate, we can hardly face the lions. However, here we're really not even talking about sacrifice. We're talking about theft. We're talking about robbing God. THE TITHE DOES NOT BELONG TO US — IT BELONGS TO GOD.

The only reason a person might believe he couldn't live on $9 out of $10 is because he doesn't have a dollar's worth of faith that God can help him. Would you sincerely like to know how to stop stealing from God? First, keep account of every dollar God gives you. Second, keep account of **his** money. Third, give it to him before you steal it. It's that simple.

THE SUBTLE GONIFF

The second kind of Goniff is somewhat more subtle. The Subtle Goniff does not steal God's purse — he steals God's purse strings, which amounts to about the same thing, but it's a more subtle form of robbery. The Subtle Goniff says he's willing to pay his full tithe, but only if he has the prerogative to dictate exactly how the money should be spent. So really, although he says he's giving to the Lord, he demands the Lord allow him to spend the Lord's money. Now if someone gives you money, but won't let you spend it, are you really being given money? No, you aren't are you? It's a subtle form of robbery.

The tithe does not belong to us. We have no inherent right to say how it should be spent. The tithe belongs to God, and he through his Spirit will dictate how it is to be used. We must take our hands off of it. So how do we stop stealing God's purse strings? First, remember that you tithe as a duty and not as a mitzveh. We don't have any choice — we either obey and tithe, or we disobey and face God our Judge. Therefore, we cannot expect to be listened to like the chairman of the board just because we tithe. Remember that your tithe belongs to God, not to you, so it's not the domain where you have the "big say." Remember also that the body of believers can determine how the tithe should be used as the Holy Spirit corporately directs them. In fact, this is precisely the Biblical pattern and God's plan, so we had better not be guilty of interfering with God by withholding our tithes as a weapon to try to dictate how the Body must operate.

THE UNWITTING GONIFF

In order to perceive the third type of goniff, we must study Malachi 3:10 which says: "Bring ye all the tithes into the storehouse that there may be meat in mine house, and prove me now herewith, said the Lord of hosts, if I will not open you the windows of heaven, and pour you out a blessing, that there will not be room enough to receive it." The passage specifically states that we are to bring all the tithes into the storehouse, that there may be "meat" in God's house. We have a specific local responsibility to keep God's house running, and we must therefore give God's tithe to one body of believers. The tithe should not be confused with the offering. The offering can be put anywhere at any time (at the Spirit's discretion). But the offering does not include the tithe — the offering is money over and above the tithe. The tithe is the basic financial support for the local body of believers to keep God's house running in that particular location. Without the tithe, all of the local congregations in the world would suffer financial catastrophe. The tithe is what keeps the lights on, what keeps the bills paid, the running expenses covered. Offerings are for extra expenses, but the tithe keeps the doors open, and we have a specific local responsibility to keep God's house running. If you are dividing your tithe in three or four or five various locations, you are flagrantly disobedient to God.

The Unwitting Goniff thinks that if he spends $1 out of $10 anywhere he wants, as long as he spends that percentage, he's being obedient to God. But the fact is that if he is not putting it all into one storehouse as God requires, then he is actually misplacing God's money, which amounts to a kind of robbery, and, to say the least, irresponsible stewardship. God's house is not just anywhere any more than our leaders are just anybody. Our leaders are only the ones to whom we are in submission. Hebrews 13:17 says "Obey your leaders." The tithe is stolen unless it is put where God demands, at the feet of the leaders of the flock (see Acts 4:35).

In the Torah we read, "You shall not muzzle a threshing ox" (Deuteronomy 25:4). Rabbi Saul picks this up in the Jewish New Covenant and applies it to the right of ministers to have a salary. He writes, "If we have sown a spiritual crop for you, is it too much to expect from you a material harvest?" (I Corinthians 9:11). "You know (do you not?) that those who perform the temple service eat the temple offerings, and those who wait upon the altar claim their share of the sacrifice. In the same way the Lord gave instructions that those who preach the Gospel should earn their living by the Gospel" (I Corinthians 9:13-14). "For the laborer is worthy of his hire" (Luke 10:7).

Therefore, each believer has a responsibility to put **all** of his tithe in the local storehouse of the Body where he is a member in order that each believer will be contributing to the salary of his own pastor. For this is Yeshua's way of supporting the full-time ministry of his servants all over the world.

In Acts 5:1-12 we read of a couple who resented Yeshua's

way of doing things. They didn't like putting very much money at their leader's feet, and they decided to lie about what they were doing. Ananias had come into a large amount of money from the sale of some property, so he told his wife, "Look honey, this is a lot of money, and we'd better not be foolish or anything. So look, Peter will never know and neither will the Holy Spirit; let's just go make a token offering and we'll be okay." So Ananias went in before Peter and he laid down a few bills, and the next thing he knew he was killed dead on the spot by the Holy Spirit. Lying or trying to fool the Holy Spirit is a very serious matter.

Now some people might have the impression that the Holy Spirit won't really know, that they don't really have to spend $1 out of $10, they don't really have to lay that kind of money at the feet of their pastors, that they can just make a token little payment here and there and it will be all right. But the fact of the matter is that the Holy Spirit is not fooled, and it's very dangerous to think that he is. Yeshua is not fooled, either. He looks at the books of our Messianic synagogue and he can see that many of the people are not tithing to our synagogue. They are robbing God. He sees these people running around to meetings everywhere, but where are they in submission, and where is their tithe going — at whose feet are they putting God's money? Or is God's tithe being broken up and scattered all around, until it's so small and so diffused and diluted that it is insufficient to keep "meat" in the Lord's house? Is God's tithe being treated like a pie that has been sliced so many ways it won't feed anybody?

Yeshua looks around and he sees Sister A and he says, "I gave Sister A $400 this month . . . where is my $40?" He looks around and he sees Brother B and he says to himself, "I gave Brother B $6,000 this month . . . where is my $600? Why isn't it being laid at the feet of the leaders to whom this man is in submission so I can use my money in a great and powerful way in the Jewish community?" Yeshua is not very impressed with thieves. Nor are the new believers who are asking themselves whether they shall obey the Lord and are looking to our example.

Here are five ways to stop stealing God's money from the local storehouse. First, stop being a floater and find a leader. Second, when you know who your leader is, then you'll know where your one-tenth is to be laid. Third, give the purse strings of God's tithes to God's sovereignly led body. Fourth, you handle only the purse strings of your offering. Fifth, don't steal from your tithes to pay any offerings.

SUMMARY

In conclusion, we must remember that tithing is not optional. We disobey God's command to tithe at our own peril. Our rationalizations may sound all right to us, but how will they sound to Yeshua? And how would they sound to all the Jewish believers who have paid with their lives in the Roman coliseum and in various other places down through the ages? When you die, you will see these people. If you're not paying your tithes, what will you say to them? How will you explain your theft of God's money? And what would have happened to the world-embracing power of the first Jewish fellowship of believers in Yeshua if these people had said, "Look, Peter, I want to be like Ananias and just make a token payment because I'm too tight to pay my tithes"?

Tithing is the believer's way of giving proof of his love (II Corinthians 8:24). Anyone can say he loves the Lord, but to offer his money for the Lord's service is his concrete way of offering love and worship to the Lord. His reluctance to give is an indicator of the degree of his love (see James 2:15-17).

Because he has given everything to us, even his life's blood, we owe everything to him. Therefore, he gives us the privilege of proving our love for him by freely, generously, but without ostentation (Matthew 6:1-4; Mark 12:41-44), giving of our very substance to him as a token of our whole beings which we gladly own are his alone.

Each Lord's Day we concretely dedicate ourselves to the Lord by giving back to him in the tithe a portion of all that he has given to us. In this way we give him ourselves (II Corinthians 8:5). Our money is a token of our self-giving to him, even as the broken matzoh and the wine are tokens of his infinitely greater self-giving for us and our eternal well-being.

Money is part of our substance, the very fruit of our toil and the residue of our spent life's time. When we worship God with our finances, we are confirming the sincerity of our love for him; we are, so to speak, putting our money where our mouth is, and showing him **real** sacrificial love, not mere lip service. Therefore, when we bring the money set aside in

our budget and lay it at the Lord's feet on the Lord's Day, it
is an act of worship, not a grudging duty, and we rejoice that
God has prospered us so that we have the privilege of contributing to our synagogue tithe box.

Whenever we give money in our synagogues, it is worship.
It is worship when we put our tithe in an envelope, holding it
in our hand and praying over it before we pass the envelope
to the shamosh in the aisle. It is worship when we take our
offering to the foot of the bimah (pulpit) to dedicate ourselves and our substance to the Lord. When offered in love,
our money is a pleasing sacrifice to the Lord, a test of faith,
yet a joyful praise offering to God. Tithing is worship.

"My children, love must not be a matter of words or talk;
it must be genuine, and show itself in action" (I John 3:18).
"Do not neglect to do good and share what you have, for
such sacrifices are pleasing to God" (Hebrews 13:16). *(NEB)*

The first Jewish believers in Yeshua saw their unique role
in Jewish history and seized the opportunity to win the world
for Yeshua Ha Mashiach and they threw their whole weight,
financially and even with their blood, into the task. The
question is, will we also throw our weight into the task? Will
we systematically pay our tithes in faith that God will meet
our own financial needs because we are being obedient to
him? Will we rejoice as we see God make his promise in
Malachi 3:10 a reality in our lives: "Prove me now therewith,
saith the Lord of Host, if I will not open you the windows of
heaven and pour you out a blessing that there will not be
room enough to receive it?"

Therefore, let this teaching on tithing be a stumbling block
to none. "For if there is an eager willingness to give, God
accepts what a man has; he does not ask for what a man
does not have (II Corinthians 8:12). So then, as we have
opportunity, let us do good to all men, and especially to
those who are of the household of faith" (Galatians 6:10).

God of Israel,

Thank you for calling me to a unique destiny in Jewish history. Thank you for the hundreds of Jewish souls you will bring into your Kingdom through the finances you have entrusted to me.

Lord, forgive me if I have ever stolen your tithe.

Lord, forgive me if I have ever arrogantly tried to dictate how you should spend your money instead of trusting your wisdom and the wisdom of the God-appointed leadership of the Body to whom I belong.

Lord, forgive me if I have not brought all my tithe into your local storehouse, committing its use to the Body of believers to whom I am in submission and with whom I am a disciple.

Lord, I promise not only to tithe, but to tithe as YOU COMMAND in your Word, without dictating how you are to spend your money, and without scattering your tithe in as many storehouses as I please but only after the New Covenant pattern, that is, into the local storehouse of the Body in which I feel God has placed me.

In Yeshua's Name,
Amen.

Signed _____

NOTE: WHEN YOU ADD YOUR SIGNATURE TO MAKE THIS YOUR PRAYER OF REPENTANCE AND COMMITMENT TO THE LORD, DO NOT RETURN THIS DECLARATION TO THE OFFICE BUT KEEP IT AS A REMINDER LEST YOU SIN AGAIN.

A Messianic Erev Shabbat Service

Like the first Jewish believers in Yeshua, we who are adherents of Messianic Judaism do not fail to acknowledge both the Sabbath and the Lord's Day. By meeting not only on Sunday but also on Friday night, Jewish believers point to the continuity of their Jewish faith, preserving both its past and its future as they witness to the fullness of their Judaism for the benefit of the salvation of their local Jewish community.

Note: In Yeshua's time there was opportunity for free prayer along with the synagogue fixed prayers.

Contents

A MESSIANIC EREV SHABBAT SERVICE

*These page numbers refer to those at the bottom.

PRAYER ON ENTERING THE SYNAGOGUE

vah-ah-nee b'rohv chahs-d'chah ah-voh vey-teh-chah ehsh-tah-chah-veh
ehl hey-chahl kahd-sh'chah b'yeer-ah-teh-chah. mah toh-voo oh-hah-leh-
chah yah-ah-kohv meesh-k'noh-teh-chah yis-ra-el. vah-ah-nee b-rohv
chahs-d'chah ah-voh vey-teh-chah ehsh-tah-cha-veh ehl hey-chal kad-
sh'chah b'yeer-ah-teh-chah. ah-doh-nye ah-hahv-tee m'ohn bay-teh-chah
oo-m'kohm meesh-kahn k'voh-deh-chah. vah-ah-nee esh-tah-chah-veh
v-ech-rah-ah ev'r'chah leef-nay ah-doh-nye oh-see. vah-ah-nee t'fee-la-tee
l'chah ah-doh-nye et rah-tsohn elo-heem. b'rahv chas-deh-chah ah-ney-
nee beh-eh-met yish-eh-cha.

As for me, in the abundance of thy loving kindness will I
come into thy house: I will worship toward thy holy temple
in the fear of thee.

How goodly are thy tents, O Jacob, thy tabernacles, O
Israel! As for me, in the abundance of thy loving kindness
will I come into thy house: I will worship toward thy holy
temple in the fear of thee. Lord, I love the habitation of thy
house and the place where thy glory dwelleth. As for me, I
will worship and bow down: I will bend the knee before the
Lord, my maker. And as for me, may my prayer unto thee,
O Lord, be in an acceptable time: O God, in the abundance
of thy loving kindness, answer me in the truth of thy salvation.

SILENT MEDITATION
PSALM 122

sah-mach-tee b'ohm-reem lee beyt adonai neh-lech. ohm-doht ha-yoo
rag-ley-noo be-shah-rye-yeech ye'roo-shah-lye-yeem. y'roo-shah-lye-yeem
hah-b'noo-yah k'eer sheh-choo-brah lah yach-dahv. sheh-shahm ah-loo
sh-vah-teem sheev-tay yah ay-doot l-yees-ra-el l-hoh-doht l-shem ah-do-
nye. kee shah-mah yahsh-voo kee-soht l'meesh-paht kee-soht l'vayt dah-
veed. shah-ah-loo sha-lom y-roo-shah-lye-yeem yeesh-lah-yoo oh-hah-vah-
yeech. y'hee sha-lom b'chay-lech shal-vah b'ahr-m'noh-tah-yeech. l'mah-
ahn ah-chye v'ray-eye ah-dahb'rah nah sha-lom bach. l'mah-ahn beyt ah-
do-nye eh-lo-hey-noo ah-vah-k'shah tohv lahch.

I was glad when they said unto me, let us go into the
house of the Lord. Our feet shall stand within thy gates, O
Jerusalem. Jerusalem is builded as a city that is compact
together: whither the tribes go up, the tribes of the Lord,
unto the testimony of Israel, to give thanks unto the name
of the Lord. For there are set thrones of judgment, the thrones
of the house of David. Pray for the peace of Jerusalem: they
shall prosper that love thee. Peace be within thy walls, and
prosperity within thy palaces. For my brethren and com-
panions' sakes, I will now say, peace be within thee. Because
of the house of the Lord our God I will seek thy good.

PRAYER ON ENTERING THE SYNAGOGUE

וַאֲנִי בְּרֹב חַסְדְּךָ אָבוֹא בֵיתֶךָ
אֶשְׁתַּחֲוֶה אֶל־הֵיכַל קָדְשְׁךָ בְּיִרְאָתֶךָ:

מַה־טֹּבוּ אֹהָלֶיךָ יַעֲקֹב מִשְׁכְּנֹתֶיךָ יִשְׂרָאֵל: וַאֲנִי
בְּרֹב חַסְדְּךָ אָבוֹא בֵיתֶךָ אֶשְׁתַּחֲוֶה אֶל־הֵיכַל
קָדְשְׁךָ בְּיִרְאָתֶךָ: יְיָ אָהַבְתִּי מְעוֹן בֵּיתֶךָ וּמְקוֹם
מִשְׁכַּן כְּבוֹדֶךָ: וַאֲנִי אֶשְׁתַּחֲוֶה וְאֶכְרָעָה אֶבְרְכָה
לִפְנֵי־יְיָ עֹשִׂי: וַאֲנִי תְפִלָּתִי לְךָ יְיָ עֵת רָצוֹן אֱלֹהִים
בְּרָב־חַסְדֶּךָ עֲנֵנִי בֶּאֱמֶת יִשְׁעֶךָ:

SILENT MEDITATION
PSALM 122

שָׂמַחְתִּי בְּאֹמְרִים לִי בֵּית יְהֹוָה נֵלֵךְ:
עֹמְדוֹת הָיוּ רַגְלֵינוּ בִּשְׁעָרַיִךְ יְרוּשָׁלָ͏ִם:
יְרוּשָׁלַ͏ִם הַבְּנוּיָה כְּעִיר שֶׁחֻבְּרָה־לָּהּ
יַחְדָּו: שֶׁשָּׁם עָלוּ שְׁבָטִים שִׁבְטֵי־יָהּ
עֵדוּת לְיִשְׂרָאֵל לְהֹדוֹת לְשֵׁם יְהֹוָה:
כִּי שָׁמָּה ׀ יָשְׁבוּ כִסְאוֹת לְמִשְׁפָּט
כִּסְאוֹת לְבֵית דָּוִד: שַׁאֲלוּ שְׁלוֹם
יְרוּשָׁלָ͏ִם יִשְׁלָיוּ אֹהֲבָיִךְ: יְהִי־שָׁלוֹם
בְּחֵילֵךְ שַׁלְוָה בְּאַרְמְנוֹתָיִךְ: לְמַעַן
אַחַי וְרֵעָי אֲדַבְּרָה־נָּא שָׁלוֹם בָּךְ:
לְמַעַן בֵּית־יְהֹוָה אֱלֹהֵינוּ אֲבַקְשָׁה טוֹב
לָךְ:

97

BENEDICTION ON KINDLING THE SABBATH-LIGHT

bah-rooch ah-tah ah-doh-nye elo-hey-noo meh-lech hah-oh-lahm ah-sher
kid-shah-noo b'mitz-voh-tahv v'tsi-vah-noo l'had-leek ner shel shah-baht.

Blessed art thou, O Lord our God, King of the universe,
who hast sanctified us by thy commandments, and hast commanded us to kindle the Sabbath-light.

BENEDICTION ON KINDLING THE FESTIVAL-LIGHT

bah-rooch ah-tah ah-do-noy elo-hey-noo me-lech ha-olahm a-sher kee
d'-shah-noo b-meetz-voh-tahv v'tsee-vah-noo l'hahd-leek ner shel (shab-
baht vah) yohm-tohv.

Blessed art thou, O Lord our God, King of the universe,
who hast sanctified us by thy commandments, and hast commanded us to kindle the Festival-light.

On the first night of the Festival, add the following:

bah-rooch ah-tah ah-do-noy elo-hey-noo me-lech ha-olahm she-he-ch'yah-
noo v'kee-y'mah-noo vuh-hee-gee-ah-noo lahz-mahn ha-zeh.

Blessed art thou, O Lord our God, King of the universe,
who hast kept us in life, and hast preserved us, and hast
enabled us to reach this season.

SHALOM ALECHEM

sha-lom a-le-chem mal-a-chey ha-sha-ret mal-a-chey el-yohn mee-mel-ech
mal-chey ham'-la-cheem ha-ka-dosh bah-rooch hoo. bo-a-chem l'sha-lom
mal-a-chey ha-sha-lom mal-a-chey el-yon. mee-meh-lech mal-chey ham'la-
cheem ha-ka-dohsh bah-rooch hoo. bar-choo-nee l'sha-lom mal-a-chey
ha-sha-lom mal-a-chey el-yohn mee-meh-lech mal-chey ham'la-cheem
ha-ka-dohsh bah-rooch hoo. tzet-chem l'sha-lom mal-a-chey ha-sha-lom
mal-a-chey el-yon mee-meh-lech mal-chey ham'la-cheem ha-ka-dohsh
ba-rooch hoo.

Peace be with you, ministering angels,
  Messengers of the Most High,
  The King of Kings
  The Holy One, blessed be he.*

May your coming be in peace, etc.
  (*repeat)

Bless me with peace, etc.
  (*repeat)

May your going be in peace, etc.
  (*repeat)

BENEDICTION ON KINDLING THE SABBATH-LIGHT

בָּרוּךְ אַתָּה יְיָ, אֱלֹהֵינוּ מֶלֶךְ הָעוֹלָם, אֲשֶׁר קִדְּשָׁנוּ
בְּמִצְוֹתָיו, וְצִוָּנוּ לְהַדְלִיק נֵר שֶׁל־שַׁבָּת:

BENEDICTION ON KINDLING THE FESTIVAL-LIGHT

בָּרוּךְ אַתָּה יְיָ, אֱלֹהֵינוּ מֶלֶךְ הָעוֹלָם, אֲשֶׁר קִדְּשָׁנוּ
בְּמִצְוֹתָיו, וְצִוָּנוּ לְהַדְלִיק נֵר שֶׁל (בערב שבת שַׁבָּת וְ)
יוֹם טוֹב:

On the first night of the Festival, add the following:

בָּרוּךְ אַתָּה יְיָ, אֱלֹהֵינוּ מֶלֶךְ הָעוֹלָם, שֶׁהֶחֱיָנוּ,
וְקִיְּמָנוּ, וְהִגִּיעָנוּ לַזְּמַן הַזֶּה:

SHALOM ALECHEM

שָׁלוֹם עֲלֵיכֶם מַלְאֲכֵי הַשָּׁרֵת מַלְאֲכֵי
עֶלְיוֹן מִמֶּלֶךְ מַלְכֵי הַמְּלָכִים הַקָּדוֹשׁ בָּרוּךְ
הוּא : פ"ג

בּוֹאֲכֶם לְשָׁלוֹם מַלְאֲכֵי הַשָּׁלוֹם מַלְאֲכֵי
עֶלְיוֹן מִמֶּלֶךְ מַלְכֵי הַמְּלָכִים הַקָּדוֹשׁ בָּרוּךְ
הוּא : פ"ג

בָּרְכוּנִי לְשָׁלוֹם מַלְאֲכֵי הַשָּׁלוֹם מַלְאֲכֵי
עֶלְיוֹן מִמֶּלֶךְ מַלְכֵי הַמְּלָכִים הַקָּדוֹשׁ בָּרוּךְ
הוּא : פ"ג

צֵאתְכֶם לְשָׁלוֹם מַלְאֲכֵי הַשָּׁלוֹם מַלְאֲכֵי
עֶלְיוֹן מִמֶּלֶךְ מַלְכֵי הַמְּלָכִים הַקָּדוֹשׁ בָּרוּךְ
הוּא : פ"ג

99

LECHAH DODI

l'chah doh-dee leek-raht cah-lah p'nay shab-baht n'kah-b'lah: sh'mohr
v'zah-chor b'dee-boor eh-chad. heesh-mee-ah-noo el ha-m'yoo-chad ah-
do-nye echad oo'sh'moh echad l'shem oo-l'teef-eh-ret v'leet-hee-lah.
leek-raht shab-baht l'choo v'nayl-chah kee hee m'kohr hah-b'rah-chah
may-rohsh mee-keh-dem n'soo-chah sohf mah-ah-seh b'mah-cha-shah-
vah t'chee-lah. meek-dahsh meh-lech eer m'loo-chah koo-mee ts'ee mee-
tohch hah-hah-feh-chah rahv lach she-vet b'eh-mek hah-bah-chah v'hoo
yah-chah-mohl ah-lye-yeech chem-lah. heet-nah-ah-ree meh-ah-far koo-
mee leev-shee beeg-day teef-ahr-taych ah-mee ahl-yahd ben yee-shye
bayt hah-lach-mee kar-vah ehl naf-shee g'ah-lah. hit-oh-rah-ree^{2}kee vah
oh-rech koo-mee oh-ree oo-ree oo-ree sheer dah-ber-ee k'vohd ah-do-nye
ah-lye-yeech neeg-lah. loh tev-shee v'loh teek-ahl-mee mah teesh-toh-
chah-chee oo-mah teh-heh-mee bach yeh-che-soo ah-ne-yay ah-mee
v'niv-n'tah eer ahl tee-lah. v'hah-yoo leem-she-sah sh'oh-sah-yeech v'rah-
cha-koo kol m'vahl-ah-yeech yah-sees ah-lye-yeech elo-hah-yeech keem-
sohs cha-tahn ahl kah-lah. yah-meen oo-s'mohl teef-roh-tsee v'et ah-doh-
nye tah-ah-ree-tsee ahl yahd eesh ben pahr-tsee v'nees-m'chah v'nah-gee-
lah. boh-ee v'sha-lom ah-teh-ret bah-lah gahm b'seem-chah oo-v'tsah-
hah-lah toch eh-moo-nay ahm s'goo-lah boh-ee cha-lah boh-ee cha-lah.

Come, my friend, to meet the bride, let us welcome the
presence of the Sabbath.

"Observe" and "Remember the Sabbath day," the only
God caused us to hear in a single utterance: the Lord is One,
and his name is One to his renown and his glory and his
praise. (Come, etc.)

Come, let us go to meet the Sabbath, for it is a wellspring
of blessing; from the beginning, from of old it was ordained —
last in production, first in thought. (Come, etc.)

O sanctuary of our King, O regal city, arise, go forth from thy
overthrow; long enough hast thou dwelt in the valley of weep-
ing; verily he will have compassion upon thee. (Come, etc.)

Shake thyself from the dust, arise, put on the garments of
thy glory, O my people! Through the son of Jesse, the Bethle-
hemite, draw thou nigh unto my soul, redeem it. (Come, etc.)

Arouse thyself, arouse thyself, for thy light is come: arise,
shine; awake, awake; give forth a song; the glory of the Lord
is revealed upon thee. (Come, etc.)

Be not ashamed, neither be confounded. Why art thou cast
down, and why art thou disquieted? The poor of my people
trust in thee, and the city shall be builded on her own mound.
(Come, etc.)

And they that spoil thee shall be a spoil, and all that would
swallow thee shall be far away: thy God shall rejoice over thee,
as a bridegroom rejoiceth over his bride. (Come, etc.)

Thou shalt spread abroad on the right hand and on the
left, and thou shalt reverence the Lord. Through the offspring
of Perez we also shall rejoice and be glad. (Come, etc.)

LECHAH DODI

לְכָה דוֹדִי לִקְרַאת כַּלָּה. פְּנֵי שַׁבָּת נְקַבְּלָה: לכה

שָׁמוֹר וְזָכוֹר בְּדִבּוּר אֶחָד . הִשְׁמִיעָנוּ אֵל הַמְיֻחָד . יְיָ
אֶחָד וּשְׁמוֹ אֶחָד . לְשֵׁם וּלְתִפְאֶרֶת וְלִתְהִלָּה: לכה

לִקְרַאת שַׁבָּת לְכוּ וְנֵלְכָה. כִּי הִיא מְקוֹר הַבְּרָכָה. מֵרֹאשׁ
מִקֶּדֶם נְסוּכָה . סוֹף מַעֲשֶׂה בְּמַחֲשָׁבָה תְּחִלָּה : לכה

מִקְדַּשׁ מֶלֶךְ עִיר מְלוּכָה. קוּמִי צְאִי מִתּוֹךְ הַהֲפֵכָה. רַב
לָךְ שֶׁבֶת בְּעֵמֶק הַבָּכָא. וְהוּא יַחֲמוֹל עָלַיִךְ חֶמְלָה: לכה

הִתְנַעֲרִי מֵעָפָר קוּמִי. לִבְשִׁי בִּגְדֵי תִפְאַרְתֵּךְ עַמִּי. עַל יַד
בֶּן יִשַׁי בֵּית הַלַּחְמִי. קָרְבָה אֶל נַפְשִׁי גְאָלָהּ: לכה

הִתְעוֹרְרִי הִתְעוֹרְרִי . כִּי בָא אוֹרֵךְ קוּמִי אוֹרִי . עוּרִי
עוּרִי שִׁיר דַּבֵּרִי . כְּבוֹד יְיָ עָלַיִךְ נִגְלָה: לכה

לֹא תֵבֹשִׁי וְלֹא תִכָּלְמִי. מַה תִּשְׁתּוֹחֲחִי וּמַה תֶּהֱמִי. בָּךְ
יֶחֱסוּ עֲנִיֵּי עַמִּי . וְנִבְנְתָה עִיר עַל תִּלָּהּ:   לכה

וְהָיוּ לִמְשִׁסָּה שֹׁאסָיִךְ . וְרָחֲקוּ כָּל מְבַלְּעָיִךְ . יָשִׂישׂ
עָלַיִךְ אֱלֹהָיִךְ . כִּמְשׂוֹשׂ חָתָן עַל כַּלָּה :   לכה

יָמִין וּשְׂמֹאל תִּפְרוֹצִי . וְאֶת יְיָ תַּעֲרִיצִי . עַל יַד אִישׁ
בֶּן פַּרְצִי . וְנִשְׂמְחָה וְנָגִילָה: לכה

בּוֹאִי בְשָׁלוֹם עֲטֶרֶת בַּעְלָהּ. גַּם בְּשִׂמְחָה וּבְצָהֳלָה,
תּוֹךְ אֱמוּנֵי עַם סְגֻלָּה. בּוֹאִי כַלָּה. בּוֹאִי כַלָּה: לכה

(Lechah Dodi continued)

Come in peace, thou crown of thy husband, with rejoicing
and with cheerfulness, in the midst of the faithful of the chosen
people: come, O bride; come, O bride. (Come, etc.)

PSALM 96

sheer-oo lah-doh-nye sheer cha-dahsh sheer-oo lah-doh-nye kol ha-ah-
retz. sheer-oo lah-doh-nye bahr-choo sh'moh bas-roo mee-yohm l'yohm
ye-shua-toh. sahp-roo vah-goy-eem k'voh-doh b'chol ha-ah-meem neef-
l'oh-tahv. kee gah-dohl ah-doh-nye oo-m'hoo-lahl m'ohd noh-rah hoo
ahl kol elo-heem. kee kol ehl-hay ha-ah-meem eh-lee-leem vah-doh-nye
shah-my-eem ah-sah. hohd v'hah-dahr l'fah-nahv ohz v'teef-eh-ret b'mik-
dah-shoh. hah-voo lah-doh-nye meech-p'choht ah-meem hah-voo lah-
doh-nye k'vohd v'ohz. hah-voo lah-doh-nye k'vohd sh'moh s'oo meen-
chah oo-voh-oo l'chats-roh-tav. heesh-tah-cha-voo lah-doh-nye b'had-
raht koh-desh chee-loo me-pahn-ahv kol hah-ah-retz. eem-roo vah-goy-
eem ah-doh-nye mah-lach ahf tee-kohn te-vel bahl tee-moht yah-deen
ah-meem b'may-shah-reem. yees-m'choo hah-shah-ma-yeem v'tah-gel hah-
ah-retz yeer-ahm hah-yahm oo-m'loh-oh. yah-ah-lohz sah-dye v'chol ah-
sher boh ahz y'rah-n'noo koh ah-tsay yah-ar. leef-nay ah-doh-nye kee vah
kee vah leesh-poht hah-ah-retz yish-poht teh-vel b'tse-dek v'ah-meem
beh-eh-moo-nah-toh.

O sing unto the Lord a new song: sing unto the Lord, all
the earth. Sing unto the Lord, bless his name; show forth his
salvation from day to day. Declare his glory among the
heathen, his wonders among all people. For the Lord is great,
and greatly to be praised: he is to be feared above all gods.
For all the gods of the nations are idols: but the Lord made
the heavens. Honor and majesty are before him: strength and
beauty are in his sanctuary. Give unto the Lord, O ye kindreds
of the people, give unto the Lord glory and strength. Give
unto the Lord the glory due unto his name: bring an offering,
and come into his courts. O worship the Lord in the beauty
of holiness: fear before him, all the earth. Say among the
heathen that the Lord reigneth: the world also shall be established that it shall not be moved: he shall judge the people
righteously. Let the heavens rejoice, and let the earth be glad;
let the sea roar, and the fullness thereof. Let the field be joyful, and all that is therein: then shall all the trees of the wood
rejoice before the Lord: for he cometh, for he cometh to
judge the earth: he shall judge the world with righteousness
and the people with his truth.

PSALM 96

שִׁירוּ לַיהֹוָה שִׁיר חָדָשׁ שִׁירוּ לַיהֹוָה
כָּל־הָאָרֶץ: שִׁירוּ לַיהֹוָה בָּרְכוּ שְׁמוֹ
בַּשְּׂרוּ מִיּוֹם־לְיוֹם יְשׁוּעָתוֹ: סַפְּרוּ
בַגּוֹיִם כְּבוֹדוֹ בְּכָל־הָעַמִּים נִפְלְאוֹתָיו:
כִּי גָדוֹל יְהֹוָה וּמְהֻלָּל מְאֹד נוֹרָא
הוּא עַל־כָּל־אֱלֹהִים: כִּי ׀ כָּל־אֱלֹהֵי
הָעַמִּים אֱלִילִים וַיהֹוָה שָׁמַיִם עָשָׂה:
הוֹד־וְהָדָר לְפָנָיו עֹז וְתִפְאֶרֶת
בְּמִקְדָּשׁוֹ: הָבוּ לַיהֹוָה מִשְׁפְּחוֹת
עַמִּים הָבוּ לַיהֹוָה כָּבוֹד וָעֹז: הָבוּ
לַיהֹוָה כְּבוֹד שְׁמוֹ שְׂאוּ־מִנְחָה וּבֹאוּ
לְחַצְרוֹתָיו: הִשְׁתַּחֲווּ לַיהֹוָה בְּהַדְרַת־
קֹדֶשׁ חִילוּ מִפָּנָיו כָּל־הָאָרֶץ: אִמְרוּ
בַגּוֹיִם ׀ יְהֹוָה מָלָךְ אַף־תִּכּוֹן תֵּבֵל בַּל־
תִּמּוֹט יָדִין עַמִּים בְּמֵישָׁרִים: יִשְׂמְחוּ
הַשָּׁמַיִם וְתָגֵל הָאָרֶץ יִרְעַם הַיָּם
וּמְלֹאוֹ: יַעֲלֹז שָׂדַי וְכָל־אֲשֶׁר־בּוֹ אָז
יְרַנְּנוּ כָּל־עֲצֵי־יָעַר: לִפְנֵי יְהֹוָה ׀ כִּי בָא
כִּי בָא לִשְׁפֹּט הָאָרֶץ יִשְׁפֹּט תֵּבֵל
בְּצֶדֶק וְעַמִּים בֶּאֱמוּנָתוֹ:

103

PSALM 92

tov l'hoh-doht lah-doh-nye oo-l'zah-mer l'shem-cha ahl-yohn. l'hah-geed
bah-boh-ker chas-deh-cha ve-eh-moo-nah-t'chah bah-lay-loht. ah-lay ah-
sohr vah-al-lay nah-vel ah-lay hee-gah-yohn b'chee-nohr. kee seem-mach-
tah-nee ah-doh-nye b'fah-ah-leh-chah b'mah-ah-say yah-deh-chah ah-rah-
nen. mah gahd-loo mah-ah-seh-chah ah-doh-nye m'ohd ahm-koo mahch-
sh'voh-teh-chah. eesh bah-ahr lo yay-dah oo-che-seel loh yah-veen et
zoht. beef-roh-ach r'sha-eem k'moh ay-sev vah-yah-tsee-tsoo kol poh-ah-
lay ah-ven l'he-sham-dahm ah-day ahd. v'ah-tah mah-rohm l'oh-lam ah-
doh-nye kee he-neh oh-y'veh-cha ah-doh-nye kee-he-neh oh-y'veh-cha
yoh-veh-doo yeet-pahr-doo kol poh-ah-lay ah-ven. vah-tah-rem keer-aym
kar-nee bah-loh-tee b'sheh-men rah-ah-nahn. vah-tah-beht ay-nee b'shoo-
rye bah-kah-meem ah-lye m'reh-eem teesh-mah-nah ahz-nye. tsa-deek
kah-tah-mahr yeef-rach k'eh-rez bahl-vahn-nohn yees-geh. sh'too leem
b'vayt ah-doh-nye b'chats-roht eh-loh-hey-noo. yahf-ree-choo. ohd y'noo-
voon b'say-vah d'shay-neem v'rah-ah-nah-neem yee-yoo. l'hah-geed kee
yah-shar ah-doh-nye tsroo-ree v'loh ahv-lah-tah boh.

It is a good thing to give thanks unto the Lord, and to sing
praises unto thy name, O Most High: to show forth thy lovingkindness in the morning, and thy faithfulness every night upon
an instrument of ten strings, and upon the psaltery; upon the
harp with a solemn sound. For thou, Lord, hast made me
glad through thy work: I will triumph in the works of thy
hands. O Lord, how great are thy works! and thy thoughts are
very deep. A brutish man knoweth not; neither doth a fool
understand this. When the wicked spring as the grass, and
when all the workers of iniquity do flourish, it is that they
shall be destroyed forever: but thou, Lord, art most high for
evermore. For lo, thine enemies, O Lord, for lo, thine enemies
shall perish; all the workers of iniquity shall be scattered. But
my horn shalt thou exalt like the horn of a unicorn: I shall be
anointed with fresh oil. Mine eye also shall see my desire on
mine enemies, and mine ears shall hear my desire of the
wicked that rise up against me. The righteous shall flourish
like the palm tree: he shall grow like a cedar in Lebanon.
Those that be planted in the house of the Lord shall flourish
in the courts of our God. They shall still bring forth fruit in
old age; they shall be fat and flourishing; to show that the
Lord is upright: he is my rock, and there is no unrighteousness in him.

PSALM 92

טוֹב לְהֹדוֹת לַיהוָה וּלְזַמֵּר לְשִׁמְךָ
עֶלְיוֹן: לְהַגִּיד בַּבֹּקֶר חַסְדֶּךָ וֶאֱמוּנָתְךָ
בַּלֵּילוֹת: עֲלֵי־עָשׂוֹר וַעֲלֵי־נָבֶל עֲלֵי
הִגָּיוֹן בְּכִנּוֹר: כִּי שִׂמַּחְתַּנִי יְהוָה
בְּפָעֳלֶךָ בְּמַעֲשֵׂי יָדֶיךָ אֲרַנֵּן: מַה־גָּדְלוּ
מַעֲשֶׂיךָ יְהוָה מְאֹד עָמְקוּ מַחְשְׁבֹתֶיךָ:
אִישׁ־בַּעַר לֹא יֵדָע וּכְסִיל לֹא יָבִין
אֶת־זֹאת: בִּפְרֹחַ רְשָׁעִים ׀ כְּמוֹ עֵשֶׂב
וַיָּצִיצוּ כָּל־פֹּעֲלֵי אָוֶן לְהִשָּׁמְדָם
עֲדֵי־עַד: וְאַתָּה מָרוֹם לְעֹלָם יְהוָה: כִּי
הִנֵּה אֹיְבֶיךָ ׀ יְהוָה כִּי־הִנֵּה אֹיְבֶיךָ
יֹאבֵדוּ יִתְפָּרְדוּ כָּל־פֹּעֲלֵי אָוֶן: וַתָּרֶם
בִּרְאֵים קַרְנִי בַּלֹּתִי בְּשֶׁמֶן רַעֲנָן:
וַתַּבֵּט עֵינִי בְּשׁוּרָי בַּקָּמִים עָלַי מְרֵעִים
תִּשְׁמַעְנָה אָזְנָי: צַדִּיק כַּתָּמָר יִפְרָח
כְּאֶרֶז בַּלְּבָנוֹן יִשְׂגֶּה: שְׁתוּלִים בְּבֵית
יְהוָה בְּחַצְרוֹת אֱלֹהֵינוּ יַפְרִיחוּ: עוֹד
יְנוּבוּן בְּשֵׂיבָה דְּשֵׁנִים וְרַעֲנַנִּים יִהְיוּ:
לְהַגִּיד כִּי־יָשָׁר יְהוָה צוּרִי וְלֹא־עַלְתָה
בּוֹ:

PSALM 93

ah-doh-nye mah-lach gay-oot lah-vesh lah-vesh ah-doh-nye ohz heet-ah-
zahr ahf tee-kohn teh-vel bahl tee-moht. nah-chohn kees-ah-cha meh-ahz
meh-oh-lahm ah-tah. nahs-oo n'hah-roht ah-doh-nye nahs-oo n'hah-roht
koh-lahm yees-oo n'hah-roht dach-yahm. mee-kohl-oht may-eem rah-
beem ah-dee-reem meesh-b'ray-yahm ah-deer bah-ma-rohm ah-doh-nye
ay-doh-teh-cha neh-em-noo m'ohd l'vay-t'cha nah-ah-vah koh-desh ah-
doh-nye l'oh rech yah-meem.

The Lord reigneth, he is clothed with majesty; the Lord is
clothed with strength, wherewith he hath girded himself: the
world also is stablished, that it cannot be moved. Thy throne
is established of old: thou art from everlasting. The floods
have lifted up their voice; the floods lift up their waves. The
Lord on high is mightier than the noise of many waters, yea,
than the mighty waves of the sea. Thy testimonies are very
sure: holiness becometh thine house, O Lord, for ever.

THE INVOCATION TO PRAYER

The Reader:
bar-choo et ah-doh-nye ha-m'voh-rech.

Bless ye the Lord who is to be blessed.

The Congregation:
bah-rooch ah-doh-nye hah-m voh-rahch lee-lahm-vah-ed. bah-rooch atah
ah-doh-nye elo-hey-noo me-lech ha-olahm ah-sher bid-vah-roh ma-ah-
reev ah-rah-veem b'chach-mah poh-tey-ach sh'ahr-eem oo-veet-voo-nah
m'shah-neh ee-teem oo-mach-ah-leef et haz-mah-neem oo-m'sah-dehr et
ha-koh-cha-veem b'mish-m'roh-tay-hem bah-rah-kee-ah kir-tsoh-noh.
boh-rey yohm v'lye-lah goh-lehl ohr me-p'nay cho-shech v'cho-shech
me-p'nay ohr. oo-mah-ah-veer yohm oo-meh-vee lye-lah oo-mahv-deel
bayn yohm oo-vayn lye-lah. ah-doh-nye ts'vah-oht sh'moh. ayl chye
v'kah-yahm tah-mid yeem-lohch ah-ley-noo l'oh-lam vah-ed. bah-rooch
ah-tah ah-doh-nye ha-mah-ah-reev ah-rah-veem.

Blessed is the Lord who is to be blessed for ever and ever.

Blessed art thou, O Lord our God, King of the universe,
who at thy word bringest on the evening twilight, with wisdom
openest the gates of the heavens, and with understanding
changest times and variest the seasons, and arrangest the stars
in their watches in the sky, according to thy will. Thou createst
day and night; thou rollest away the light from before the
darkness, and the darkness from before the light; thou makest
the day to pass and the night to approach, and dividest the day
from the night, the Lord of hosts is thy name; a God living
and enduring continually, mayest thou reign over us for ever
and ever. Blessed art thou, O Lord, who bringest on the evening
twilight.

PSALM 93

יְהוָֹה מָלָךְ גֵּאוּת לָבֵשׁ לָבֵשׁ יְהוָֹה

עֹז הִתְאַזָּר אַף־תִּכּוֹן תֵּבֵל בַּל־תִּמּוֹט:

נָכוֹן כִּסְאֲךָ מֵאָז מֵעוֹלָם אָתָּה: נָשְׂאוּ

נְהָרוֹת ׀ יְהוָֹה נָשְׂאוּ נְהָרוֹת קוֹלָם

יִשְׂאוּ נְהָרוֹת דָּכְיָם: מִקֹּלוֹת ׀ מַיִם

רַבִּים אַדִּירִים מִשְׁבְּרֵי־יָם אַדִּיר

בַּמָּרוֹם יְהוָֹה: עֵדֹתֶיךָ ׀ נֶאֶמְנוּ מְאֹד

לְבֵיתְךָ נַאֲוָה־קֹדֶשׁ יְהוָֹה ה לְאֹרֶךְ

יָמִים:

THE INVOCATION TO PRAYER

The Reader:

בָּרְכוּ אֶת־יְיָ הַמְבֹרָךְ:

The Congregation:

בָּרוּךְ יְיָ הַמְבֹרָךְ לְעוֹלָם וָעֶד: בָּרוּךְ אַתָּה יְיָ אֱלֹהֵינוּ
מֶלֶךְ הָעוֹלָם אֲשֶׁר בִּדְבָרוֹ מַעֲרִיב עֲרָבִים בְּחָכְמָה
פּוֹתֵחַ שְׁעָרִים וּבִתְבוּנָה מְשַׁנֶּה עִתִּים וּמַחֲלִיף
אֶת־הַזְּמַנִּים וּמְסַדֵּר אֶת־הַכּוֹכָבִים בְּמִשְׁמְרוֹתֵיהֶם
בָּרָקִיעַ כִּרְצוֹנוֹ. בּוֹרֵא יוֹם וָלַיְלָה גּוֹלֵל אוֹר
מִפְּנֵי־חֹשֶׁךְ וְחֹשֶׁךְ מִפְּנֵי־אוֹר. וּמַעֲבִיר יוֹם
וּמֵבִיא לַיְלָה וּמַבְדִּיל בֵּין יוֹם וּבֵין לָיְלָה יְיָ צְבָאוֹת
שְׁמוֹ: אֵל חַי וְקַיָּם תָּמִיד יִמְלוֹךְ עָלֵינוּ לְעוֹלָם
וָעֶד: בָּרוּךְ אַתָּה יְיָ הַמַּעֲרִיב עֲרָבִים:

107

BLESSING GOD, THE TEACHER OF ISRAEL

ah-ha-vaht oh-lahm bayt yees-ra-el ahm-cha ah-hahv-tah toh-rah oo-
mitz-voht choo-keem oo-meesh-pah-teem oh-tah-noo lee-mahd-tah. ahl
keyn ah-doh-nye elo-hey-noo b'shach-bey-noo oo-v'koo-meh-noo nahs-
yach b'choo-keh-cha v'nees-mach b'deev-rey toh-rah-teh-cha oo-v'mitz-
voh-teh-cha l'oh-lahm vah-ed. kee chehm cha-yeh-noo v'oh-rech yah-
mey-noo oo-va-hem neh-geh yoh-mahm v'lye-lah. v'ah-hah-vah-t'cha
ahl tah-seer me-meh-noo l'oh-lah-meem. bah-rooch ah-tah ah-doh-nye
oh-hev ah-moh yees-rah-el.

With everlasting love thou hast loved the house of Israel,
thy people; a law and commandments, statutes and judgments
hast thou taught us. Therefore, O Lord our God, when we lie
down and when we rise up we will meditate on thy statutes;
yea, we will rejoice in the words of thy law and in thy commandments for ever; for they are our life and the length of
our days, and we will meditate on them day and night. And
mayest thou never take away thy love from us. Blessed art
thou, O Lord, who lovest thy people Israel.

THE TEN COMMANDMENTS

ah-noh-chee ah-doh-nye elo-hey-chah

I am the Lord thy God.

loh-yee-yeh l'chah elo-heem ah-chay-reem al pah-nye

Thou shalt have no other Gods before me.

loh tee-sah et shem ah-doh-nye elo-heh-chah lah-shahv

Thou shalt not take the name of the Lord thy God in vain.

zah-chor et yom ha-shah-bat l'cah-d'shoh

Remember the Sabbath Day to keep it holy.

cah-beyd et ah-vee-chah vuh-et eem-meh-cha

Honor thy father and thy mother.

loh teer-tzach

Thou shalt not murder.

loh teen-ahf

Thou shalt not commit adultery.

loh teeg-nohv

Thou shalt not steal.

lo tah-ah-neh v'ray-ah-chah aid cha-ker

Thou shalt not bear false witness against thy neighbor.

lo toch-mode

Thou shalt not covet.

BLESSING GOD, THE TEACHER OF ISRAEL

אַהֲבַת עוֹלָם בֵּית יִשְׂרָאֵל עַמְּךָ אָהָבְתָּ תּוֹרָה
וּמִצְוֹת חֻקִּים וּמִשְׁפָּטִים אוֹתָנוּ לִמַּדְתָּ, עַל־כֵּן יְיָ
אֱלֹהֵינוּ בְּשָׁכְבֵנוּ וּבְקוּמֵנוּ נָשִׂיחַ בְּחֻקֶּיךָ וְנִשְׂמַח
בְּדִבְרֵי תוֹרָתֶךָ וּבְמִצְוֹתֶיךָ לְעוֹלָם וָעֶד. כִּי הֵם
חַיֵּינוּ וְאֹרֶךְ יָמֵינוּ. וּבָהֶם נֶהְגֶּה יוֹמָם וָלַיְלָה:
וְאַהֲבָתְךָ אַל־תָּסִיר מִמֶּנּוּ לְעוֹלָמִים. בָּרוּךְ אַתָּה
יְיָ אוֹהֵב עַמּוֹ יִשְׂרָאֵל:

THE TEN COMMANDMENTS

אָנֹכִי יְהֹוָה אֱלֹהֶיךָ

לֹא־יִהְיֶה לְךָ אֱלֹהִים אֲחֵרִים עַל־פָּנָי:

לֹא תִשָּׂא אֶת־שֵׁם־יְהֹוָה אֱלֹהֶיךָ לַשָּׁוְא

זָכוֹר אֶת־יוֹם הַשַּׁבָּת לְקַדְּשׁוֹ:

כַּבֵּד אֶת־אָבִיךָ וְאֶת־אִמֶּךָ

לֹא־ תִּרְצָח:

לֹא תִּנְאָף:

לֹא תִּגְנֹב:

לֹא תַעֲנֶה בְרֵעֲךָ עֵד שָׁקֶר:

לֹא תַחְמֹד

THE SHEMA, OUR CONFESSION

sh'mah yees-rah-el ah-doh-nye elo-hey-noo ah-doh-nye echahd

Hear, O Israel: the Lord our God is one Lord.

bah-rooch shem kah-vohd mal-choo-toh l'ohlahm vah-ed

Blessed be his Name whose glorious kingdom is for ever and ever.

yeshua ha mashiach hoo ah-doh-nye

Yeshua the Messiah is Lord.

DEUTERONOMY 6:5-9

v'ah-hav-tah et a-doh-nye eloh-heh-cha b'chol l'vahv-cha oo-v'chol nahf-sh'cha oo-v'chol m'oh-deh-cha. v'ha-yoo ha-d'vah-reem hah-eh-leh ah-sher ah-noh-chee m'tsahv-cha ha-yohm ahl l'vah-veh-cha. v'she-nahn-tahm l'vah-neh-cha v'deeb-ar-tah bahm b'sheev-t'cha b'vey-teh-cha oo-v'lech-t'cha vah-deh-rech oo-v'shach-b'cha oo-v'koo-meh-cha. oo-k'shar-tahm l'oht ahl yah-deh-cha v'ha-yoo l'toh-tah-foht bayn ah-neh-cha. oo-ch'tav-tahm ahl m'zoo-zoht bay-teh-cha oo-veesh-ah-reh-cha.

And thou shalt love the Lord thy God with all thine heart, and with all thy soul, and with all thy might. And these words, which I command thee this day, shall be in thine heart: and thou shalt teach them diligently unto thy children, and shalt talk of them when thou sittest in thine house, and when thou walkest by the way, and when thou liest down, and when thou risest up. And thou shalt bind them for a sign upon thine hand, and they shall be as frontlets between thine eyes. And thou shalt write them upon the posts of thy house, and on thy gates.

THE SHEMA, OUR CONFESSION

שְׁמַע יִשְׂרָאֵל יְיָ אֱלֹהֵינוּ יְיָ אֶחָד :
בָּרוּךְ שֵׁם כְּבוֹד מַלְכוּתוֹ לְעוֹלָם וָעֶד :

יֵשׁוּעַ הַמָּשִׁיחַ הוּא אֲדֹנָי

DEUTERONOMY 6:5-9

וְאָהַבְתָּ אֵת יְהֹוָה אֱלֹהֶיךָ בְּכָל לְבָבְךָ וּבְכָל־
נַפְשְׁךָ וּבְכָל־מְאֹדֶךָ : וְהָיוּ הַדְּבָרִים הָאֵלֶּה
אֲשֶׁר אָנֹכִי מְצַוְּךָ הַיּוֹם עַל־לְבָבֶךָ : וְשִׁנַּנְתָּם
לְבָנֶיךָ וְדִבַּרְתָּ בָּם בְּשִׁבְתְּךָ בְּבֵיתֶךָ וּבְלֶכְתְּךָ
בַדֶּרֶךְ וּבְשָׁכְבְּךָ וּבְקוּמֶךָ : וּקְשַׁרְתָּם לְאוֹת
עַל־יָדֶךָ וְהָיוּ לְטֹטָפֹת בֵּין עֵינֶיךָ : וּכְתַבְתָּם
עַל־מְזֻזֹת בֵּיתֶךָ וּבִשְׁעָרֶיךָ :

111

DEUTERONOMY 11:13-21

v'ha-yah eem shah-moh-ah teesh-m'oo ehl mitz-voh-tye ah-sher ah-noh-chee m'tsah-veh et-chem ha-yom l'ah-hah-vah et ah-doh-nye elo-hey-chem oo-l'ahv-doh b'chol l'vahv-chem oo-v'chol nahf-sh'chem. v'nah-tah-tee m'tahr ar-ts'chem b'ee-toh yoh-reh oo-mahl-kosh v'ah-sahf-tah d'gah-neh-cha v'teer-sh-cha v'yeetz-ha-reh-cha. v'nah-tah-tee ay-sev b'sah-d'cha leev-hem-teh-cha v'ah-chal-tah v'sah-vah-tah. he-sham-roo lah-chem pehn yeef-teh l'vav-chem v'sahr-tehm vah-ah-vahd-tehm elo-heem ah-che-reem v'heesh-tah-cha-vee-tehm lah-hem. v'cha-rah ahf ah-do-nye bah-chem v'ah-tsahr et ha-shah-mayim v'loh ye-yeh mah-tahr v'ha-ah-dah-mah loh te-teyn et y'voo-lah va-ah-vad-tem m'hey-rah mey-ahl ha-aretz ha-toh-vah asher ah-doh-nye noh-teyn lah-chem. v'sahm-tehm et d'vah-rye eh-leh ahl l'vahv-chem v'ahl naf-sh'chem oo-k'shar-tehm oh-tahm l'oht ahl yed-chem v'ha-yoo l'toh-tah-foht bayn ay-nay-chem. v'lee-mahd-teem oh-tahm et b'nay-chem l'dah-behr bahm b'sheev-t'chah b'vay-teh-cha oov-lech-t'cha v'deh-rech oov-shach-b'cha oov-koo-mecha. oo-ch'tahv-tahm ahl m'zoo-zoht bay-teh-cha oo-veesh-a-recha. l'mah-ahn yeer-boo y'may-chem vee-v'may v'ney-chem ahl ha-ah-dah-mah ah-sher neesh-bah ah-doh-nye lah-ah-voh-tey-chem lah-tet lah-hem key-may hah-shah-ma-yim ahl ha-ah-retz.

And it shall come to pass if ye shall hearken diligently unto my commandments which I command you this day, to love the Lord your God, and to serve him with all your heart and with all your soul, that I will give you the rain of your land in his due season, the first rain and the latter rain, that thou mayest gather in thy corn, and thy wine, and thine oil. And I will send grass in thy fields for thy cattle, that thou mayest eat and be full. Take heed to yourselves, that your heart be not deceived, and ye turn aside, and serve other gods, and worship them; and then the Lord's wrath be kindled against you, and he shut up the heaven, that there be no rain, and that the land yield not her fruit; and lest ye perish quickly from off the good land which the Lord giveth you. Therefore shall ye lay up these my words in your heart and in your soul, and bind them for a sign upon your hand, that they may be as frontlets between your eyes. And ye shall teach them your children, speaking of them when thou sittest in thine house, and when thou walkest by the way, when thou liest down, and when thou risest up. And thou shalt write them upon the doorposts of thine house, and upon thy gates, that your days may be multiplied, and the days of your children, in the land which the Lord sware unto your fathers to give them, as the days of heaven upon the earth.

DEUTERONOMY 11:13-21

וְהָיָה אִם־שָׁמֹעַ תִּשְׁמְעוּ אֶל־מִצְוֹתַי אֲשֶׁר אָנֹכִי
מְצַוֶּה אֶתְכֶם הַיּוֹם לְאַהֲבָה אֶת־יְהֹוָה אֱלֹהֵיכֶם
וּלְעָבְדוֹ בְּכָל־לְבַבְכֶם וּבְכָל־נַפְשְׁכֶם: וְנָתַתִּי מְטַר־
אַרְצְכֶם בְּעִתּוֹ יוֹרֶה וּמַלְקוֹשׁ וְאָסַפְתָּ דְגָנֶךָ וְתִירֹשְׁךָ
וְיִצְהָרֶךָ: וְנָתַתִּי עֵשֶׂב בְּשָׂדְךָ לִבְהֶמְתֶּךָ וְאָכַלְתָּ
וְשָׂבָעְתָּ: הִשָּׁמְרוּ לָכֶם פֶּן־יִפְתֶּה לְבַבְכֶם וְסַרְתֶּם
וַעֲבַדְתֶּם אֱלֹהִים אֲחֵרִים וְהִשְׁתַּחֲוִיתֶם לָהֶם:
וְחָרָה אַף־יְהֹוָה בָּכֶם וְעָצַר אֶת־הַשָּׁמַיִם וְלֹא־יִהְיֶה
מָטָר וְהָאֲדָמָה לֹא תִתֵּן אֶת־יְבוּלָהּ וַאֲבַדְתֶּם מְהֵרָה
מֵעַל הָאָרֶץ הַטֹּבָה אֲשֶׁר יְהֹוָה נֹתֵן לָכֶם: וְשַׂמְתֶּם
אֶת־דְּבָרַי אֵלֶּה עַל־לְבַבְכֶם וְעַל־נַפְשְׁכֶם וּקְשַׁרְתֶּם
אֹתָם לְאוֹת עַל־יֶדְכֶם וְהָיוּ לְטוֹטָפֹת בֵּין עֵינֵיכֶם:
וְלִמַּדְתֶּם אֹתָם אֶת־בְּנֵיכֶם לְדַבֵּר בָּם בְּשִׁבְתְּךָ בְּבֵיתֶךָ
וּבְלֶכְתְּךָ בַדֶּרֶךְ וּבְשָׁכְבְּךָ וּבְקוּמֶךָ: וּכְתַבְתָּם עַל־
מְזוּזוֹת בֵּיתֶךָ וּבִשְׁעָרֶיךָ: לְמַעַן יִרְבּוּ יְמֵיכֶם וִימֵי

בְנֵיכֶם עַל הָאֲדָמָה אֲשֶׁר נִשְׁבַּע יְהֹוָה לַאֲבֹתֵיכֶם
לָתֵת לָהֶם כִּימֵי הַשָּׁמַיִם עַל־הָאָרֶץ:

NUMBERS 15:37-41

va-yoh-mer ah-doh-nye ehl moh-sheh leh-mohr: dah-ber ehl b'nai yees-
ra-el v'ah-mar-tah ah-lay-hem v'ah-soo lah-hem tsee-tseet al-kahn-fay
veeg-day-hem l'doh-roh-tahn v'naht-noo al-tsee-tseet ha-kah-nahf p'teel
t'chay-let. v'ha-yah lah-chem l'tsee-tseet oor-ee-tem oh-toh ooz-char-
tem et col meetz-oht ah-doh-nye vah-ah-see-tem oh-tahm v'loh tah-too-
roo ah-chah-ray l'vav-chem v'ah-chah-ray ay-nay-chem ah-sher ah-tem
zoh-neem ah-chah-ray-hem. l'mah-ahn teez-k'roo vah-ah-see-tem et col
mee-tzoh-tah vee-h'yee-tem k'doh-sheem lay-loh-hay-chem. ah-nee ah-
doh-nye e-loh-hay-chem a-sher hoh-tzay-tee et-chem may-eh-retz metz-
ray-yeem lee-h'yoht le-chem lay-loh-heem ah-nee ah-doh-nye elo-hay-
chem.

And the Lord spake unto Moses, saying, Speak unto the
children of Israel, and bid them that they make them fringes
in the borders of their garments, throughout their generations,
and that they put upon the fringe of the borders a ribband of
blue: and it shall be unto you for a fringe, that ye may look
upon it, and remember all the commandments of the Lord,
and do them; and that ye seek not after your own heart and
your own eyes, after which ye use to go a whoring: that ye
may remember, and do all my commandments, and be holy
unto your God. I am the Lord your God, which brought you
out of the land of Egypt, to be your God: I am the Lord your
God.

GOD OUR REDEEMER

eh-met veh-eh-moo-nah kol zoht v'kah-yahm ah-ley-noo kee hoo ah-doh-
nye elo-hey-noo v'ayn zoo-lah-toh vah-ah-nach-noo yees-rah-el ah-moh
ha-poh-dey-noo mee-yahd m'lah-cheem mahl-kay-noo hah-goh-ah-ley-
noo mee-kahf kol heh-ah-ree-tseem ha-el hah-neef-rah lah-noo meetza-
rey-noo v'hahm-shah-lem g'mool l'chol oi'y'vey nahf-shey-noo hah-oh-
seh g'doh-loht ahd ayn chey-kehr v'neef-lah-oht ahd ayn mees-pahr. hah-
sahm nahf-shey-noo bah-cha-yeem v'loh nah-tahn lah-moht rahg-ley-noo.
ha-mahd-ree-chey-noo ahl bah-moht oi-y'vay-noo vah-yah-rem kar-ney-
noo ahl kol sney-noo. ha-oh-seh lah-noo nee-seem oo-n'kah-mah b'fahr-
oh oh-toht oo-mohf-teem b'ahd-maht b'nai chahm. hah-mah-keh b'ehv-
rah-toh kol b'cho-rey meetz-rah-yeem v'yoh-tsey et ah-moh yees-ra-el
me-toh-cham l'chey-root oh-lahm. hah-mah-ah-veer bah-nahv beyn geez-
rey yahm soof et rohd-fey-hem v'et sho-ney-hem beet-hoh-moht tee-bah.
v'rah-oo vah-nahv g'voo-rah-toh sheeb-choo v'hoh-doo leesh-moh. oo-
mahl-choo-toh b'rahtz-ohn keeb-loo ah-ley-hem moh-sheh oo-v'ney yees-
rah-el l'chah ah-noo sheer-ah b'seem-chah rah-bah v'ahm-roo choo-lahm.

True and trustworthy is all this, and it is established with us
that he is the Lord our God, and there is none beside him, and
that we, Israel, are his people. It is he who redeemed us from
the hand of kings, even our King, who delivered us from the
grasp of all the terrible ones; the God, who on our behalf dealt
out punishment to our adversaries, and requited all the enemies
of our soul; who doeth great things past finding out, yea, and

114

NUMBERS 15:37-41

וַיֹּאמֶר יְהֹוָה אֶל־מֹשֶׁה לֵּאמֹר: דַּבֵּר אֶל־
בְּנֵי יִשְׂרָאֵל וְאָמַרְתָּ אֲלֵהֶם וְעָשׂוּ לָהֶם צִיצִת
עַל־כַּנְפֵי בִגְדֵיהֶם לְדֹרֹתָם וְנָתְנוּ עַל־צִיצִת
הַכָּנָף פְּתִיל תְּכֵלֶת: וְהָיָה לָכֶם לְצִיצִת
וּרְאִיתֶם אֹתוֹ וּזְכַרְתֶּם אֶת־כָּל־מִצְוֹת יְהֹוָה
וַעֲשִׂיתֶם אֹתָם וְלֹא תָתוּרוּ אַחֲרֵי לְבַבְכֶם
וְאַחֲרֵי עֵינֵיכֶם אֲשֶׁר־אַתֶּם זֹנִים אַחֲרֵיהֶם:
לְמַעַן תִּזְכְּרוּ וַעֲשִׂיתֶם אֶת־כָּל־מִצְוֹתָי וִהְיִיתֶם
קְדֹשִׁים לֵאלֹהֵיכֶם: אֲנִי יְהֹוָה אֱלֹהֵיכֶם
אֲשֶׁר הוֹצֵאתִי אֶתְכֶם מֵאֶרֶץ מִצְרַיִם לִהְיוֹת
לָכֶם לֵאלֹהִים אֲנִי יְהֹוָה אֱלֹהֵיכֶם:

GOD OUR REDEEMER

אֱמֶת וֶאֱמוּנָה כָּל־זֹאת וְקַיָּם עָלֵינוּ כִּי הוּא יְיָ
אֱלֹהֵינוּ וְאֵין זוּלָתוֹ וַאֲנַחְנוּ יִשְׂרָאֵל עַמּוֹ הַפּוֹדֵנוּ מִיַּד
מְלָכִים מַלְכֵּנוּ הַגּוֹאֲלֵנוּ מִכַּף כָּל־הֶעָרִיצִים הָאֵל
הַנִּפְרָע לָנוּ מִצָּרֵינוּ וְהַמְשַׁלֵּם גְּמוּל לְכָל־אוֹיְבֵי נַפְשֵׁנוּ
הָעֹשֶׂה גְדֹלוֹת עַד אֵין חֵקֶר וְנִפְלָאוֹת עַד־אֵין מִסְפָּר:
הַשָּׂם נַפְשֵׁנוּ בַּחַיִּים וְלֹא־נָתַן לַמּוֹט רַגְלֵנוּ. הַמַּדְרִיכֵנוּ
עַל־בָּמוֹת אוֹיְבֵינוּ וַיָּרֶם קַרְנֵנוּ עַל כָּל־שׂוֹנְאֵינוּ.

הָעֹשֶׂה לָּנוּ נִסִּים וּנְקָמָה בְּפַרְעֹה אוֹתֹת וּמוֹפְתִים
בְּאַדְמַת בְּנֵי־חָם. הַמַּכֶּה בְעֶבְרָתוֹ כָּל־בְּכוֹרֵי מִצְרַיִם
וַיּוֹצֵא אֶת־עַמּוֹ יִשְׂרָאֵל מִתּוֹכָם לְחֵרוּת עוֹלָם:
הַמַּעֲבִיר בָּנָיו בֵּין גִּזְרֵי יַם־סוּף אֶת רוֹדְפֵיהֶם וְאֶת־
שׂוֹנְאֵיהֶם בִּתְהֹמוֹת טִבַּע. וְרָאוּ בָנָיו גְּבוּרָתוֹ שִׁבְּחוּ
וְהוֹדוּ לִשְׁמוֹ. וּמַלְכוּתוֹ בְּרָצוֹן קִבְּלוּ עֲלֵיהֶם מֹשֶׁה וּבְנֵי
יִשְׂרָאֵל לְךָ עָנוּ שִׁירָה בְּשִׂמְחָה רַבָּה וְאָמְרוּ כֻלָּם:

115

(God our Redeemer continued)

wonders without number; who holdest our soul in life, and hath not suffered our feet to be moved; who made us tread upon the high places of our enemies, and exalted our horn over all them that hated us; who wrought for us miracles and vengeance upon Pharoah, signs and wonders in the land of the children of Ham; who in his wrath smote all the first-born of Egypt, and brought forth his people Israel from among them to everlasting freedom; who made his children pass between the divisions of the Red Sea, but sank their pursuers and their enemies in the depths. Then his children beheld his might; they praised and gave thanks unto his name, and willingly accepted his sovereignty. Moses and the children of Israel sang a song unto thee with great joy, saying, all of them,

MEE CHAH-MOH-CHA

mee chah-moh-cha bah-eh-leem ah-doh-nye mee chah-moh-chah neh-dahr bah-koh-desh noh-rah t'hee-loht oh-seh feh-leh. mahl-choo-t'chah rah-oo vah-neh-chah boh-key-ah yahm leef-ney moh-sheh zeh eh-lee ah-noo v'ahm-roo. ah-doh-nye yeem-lach l'oh-lam vah-ed. v'neh-eh-mahr kee fah-dah ah-doh-nye et yah-a-kohv oo-g'ah-loh mee-yahd chah-zak mee-meh-noo. bah-rooch ah-tah ah-doh-nye ga-ahl yees-rah-el.

Who is like unto thee, O Lord, among the mighty ones? Who is like unto thee, glorious in holiness, revered in praises, doing wonders?

Thy children beheld thy sovereign power, as thou didst cleave the sea before Moses: they exclaimed, this is my God! and said, the Lord shall reign for ever and ever.

And it is said, for the Lord hath delivered Jacob, and redeemed him from the hand of him that was stronger than he. Blessed art thou, O Lord, who hast redeemed Israel.

HAHSH-KEE-VEY-NOO

hahsh-kee-vey-noo ah-doh-nye eh-loh-hey-noo l'sha-lom v'hah-ah-mee-dey-noo mal-key-noo l'cha-yeem. oo-f'rohs ah-ley-noo soo-caht sh'loh-meh-chah v'tahk-ney-noo b'ay-tsah toh-vah meel'fah-neh-cha v'hoh-she-ay-noo l'mah-ahn sh'meh-chah. v'hah-gen ba-ah-dey-noo v'hah-sehr mey-ah-ley-noo oh-yev deh-vehr v'che-rev v'rah-ahv v'yah-gohn v'hah-sehr sah-tahn meel-fah-ney-noo oo-may-ah-cha-rey-noo. oo-v'tsayl k'nah-feh-chah tahs-tee-rey-noo kee ayl shohm-rey-noo oo-mah-tsee-ley-noo ah-tah kee ehl melech chah-noon v'rah-choom ah-tah. oo-sh'mohr tsey-tey-noo oo-voh-ey-noo l'chah-yeem oo-l'sha-lom mey-ah-tah v'ahd oh-lahm. oo-f'rohs ah-ley-noo soo-caht sh'loh-meh-chah. bah-rooch ah-tah ah-doh-nye hah-poh-reys soo-caht sha-lohm ah-ley-nu v'ahl kol ah-moh yees-rah-el v'ahl y'roosh-ah-la-yeem.

Cause us, O Lord our God, to lie down in peace, and raise us up, O our King, unto life. Spread over us the tabernacle of thy peace; direct us aright through thine own good counsel;

MEE CHAH-MOH-CHA

מִי־כָמֹכָה בָּאֵלִם יְהֹוָה מִי כָּמֹכָה נֶאְדָּר בַּקֹּדֶשׁ
נוֹרָא תְהִלֹּת עֹשֵׂה פֶלֶא: מַלְכוּתְךָ רָאוּ בָנֶיךָ בּוֹקֵעַ
יָם לִפְנֵי מֹשֶׁה זֶה אֵלִי עָנוּ וְאָמְרוּ:

יְיָ יִמְלֹךְ לְעֹלָם וָעֶד: וְנֶאֱמַר כִּי־פָדָה יְיָ אֶת־יַעֲקֹב
וּגְאָלוֹ מִיַּד חָזָק מִמֶּנּוּ: בָּרוּךְ אַתָּה יְיָ גָּאַל יִשְׂרָאֵל:

HAHSH-KEE-VEY-NOO

הַשְׁכִּיבֵנוּ יְיָ אֱלֹהֵינוּ לְשָׁלוֹם וְהַעֲמִידֵנוּ מַלְכֵּנוּ
לְחַיִּים. וּפְרוֹשׂ עָלֵינוּ סֻכַּת שְׁלוֹמֶךָ. וְתַקְּנֵנוּ בְּעֵצָה
טוֹבָה מִלְּפָנֶיךָ. וְהוֹשִׁיעֵנוּ לְמַעַן שְׁמֶךָ. וְהָגֵן בַּעֲדֵנוּ
וְהָסֵר מֵעָלֵינוּ אוֹיֵב דֶּבֶר וְחֶרֶב וְרָעָב וְיָגוֹן. וְהָסֵר
שָׂטָן מִלְּפָנֵינוּ וּמֵאַחֲרֵינוּ. וּבְצֵל כְּנָפֶיךָ תַּסְתִּירֵנוּ כִּי
אֵל שׁוֹמְרֵנוּ וּמַצִּילֵנוּ אָתָּה. כִּי אֵל מֶלֶךְ חַנּוּן וְרַחוּם
אָתָּה וּשְׁמוֹר צֵאתֵנוּ וּבוֹאֵנוּ לְחַיִּים וּלְשָׁלוֹם מֵעַתָּה
וְעַד עוֹלָם: וּפְרוֹשׂ עָלֵינוּ סֻכַּת שְׁלוֹמֶךָ: בָּרוּךְ
אַתָּה יְיָ הַפּוֹרֵשׂ סֻכַּת שָׁלוֹם עָלֵינוּ וְעַל כָּל־עַמּוֹ
יִשְׂרָאֵל וְעַל־יְרוּשָׁלָיִם:

(Hahsh-Kee-Vey-Noo continued)

save us for thy name's sake; be thou a shield about us; remove from us every enemy, pestilence, sword, famine and sorrow; remove also the adversary from before us and from behind us. O shelter us beneath the shadow of thy wings, for thou, O God, art our Guardian and our Deliverer; yea, thou, O God, art a gracious and merciful King; and guard our going out and our coming in unto life and unto peace from this time forth and for evermore; yea, spread over us the tabernacle of thy peace. Blessed art thou, O Lord, who spreadest the tabernacle of peace over us and over all thy people Israel, and over Jerusalem.

On Sabbaths:

v'shahm-roo b'nay yees-rah-el et hah-shah-baht lah-ah-soht et hah-shab-baht l'doh-roh-tahm b'reet oh-lahm. bay-nee oo-vayn b'nay yees-rah-el oht hee l'oh-lahm kee shey-shet yah-meem ah-sah ah-doh-nye et hah-shah-my-yeem v'et hah-ah-retz oo'v-yohm hahsh-vee-ee shab-vaht vah-yee-nah-fahsh.

And the children of Israel shall keep the Sabbath, to observe the Sabbath throughout their generations, for an everlasting covenant. It is a sign between me and the children of Israel for ever, that in six days the Lord made the heavens and the earth, and on the seventh day he rested, and ceased from his work.

On Passover, Pentecost and Tabernacles, say:

vye-dah-behr moh-sheh et m'oh-day ah-doh-nye el b'nay yees-rah-el

And Moses declared the set feasts of the Lord unto the children of Israel.

On New Year:

teek-oo vah-choh-desh sho-far bah-keh-seh l'yohm hah-gay-noo. kee chohk l'yees-rah-el hoo meesh-pot lay-loh-hay yah-ah-kohv

Blow the horn on the new moon, at the beginning of the month, for our day of festival: for it is a statute for Israel, a decree of the God of Jacob.

On the Day of Atonement:

kee vah-yohm ha-zeh y'cha-pehr ah-lay-chem l'tah-hehr et-chem. mee-kol cha-toh-tay-chem leef-nay ah-doh-nye teet-ha-roo

For on this day shall atonement be made for you to cleanse you; from all your sins shall ye be clean before the Lord.

118

On Sabbaths:

וְשָׁמְרוּ בְנֵי־יִשְׂרָאֵל אֶת־הַשַּׁבָּת לַעֲשׂוֹת אֶת־הַשַּׁבָּת
לְדֹרֹתָם בְּרִית עוֹלָם: בֵּינִי וּבֵין בְּנֵי יִשְׂרָאֵל אוֹת הִיא
לְעֹלָם כִּי־שֵׁשֶׁת יָמִים עָשָׂה יְהוָה אֶת־הַשָּׁמַיִם וְאֶת־
הָאָרֶץ וּבַיּוֹם הַשְּׁבִיעִי שָׁבַת וַיִּנָּפַשׁ:

On Passover, Pentecost and Tabernacles, say:

וַיְדַבֵּר מֹשֶׁה אֶת־מֹעֲדֵי יְיָ אֶל־בְּנֵי יִשְׂרָאֵל:

On New Year:

תִּקְעוּ בַחֹדֶשׁ שׁוֹפָר בַּכֶּסֶה לְיוֹם חַגֵּנוּ: כִּי חֹק
לְיִשְׂרָאֵל הוּא מִשְׁפָּט לֵאלֹהֵי יַעֲקֹב:

On the Day of Atonement:

כִּי־בַיּוֹם הַזֶּה יְכַפֵּר עֲלֵיכֶם לְטַהֵר אֶתְכֶם. מִכֹּל
חַטֹּאתֵיכֶם לִפְנֵי יְיָ תִּטְהָרוּ:

THE AMIDAH
The Congregation will stand for the Amidah.

ah-doh-nye s'fah-taye teef-tahch oo-fee yah-geed t'hee-lah-teh-cha. bah-
rooch ah-tah ah-doh-nye elo-hey-noo vah-loh-hey ah-voh-tay-noo, eloh-
hey ahv-rah-hahm eloh-hey yeets-chahk vay-loh-hey yah-ah-kohv, hah-
ayl hahg-dohl hah-gee-bohr v'hah-noh-rah ayl ehl-yohn, goh-mayl chah-
sah-deem toh-veem v'koh-nay ha-kohl, v'zoh-chayr chahs-day ah-voht
oo-may-vee goh-ayl leev-nay v'nay-hem l'mah-ahn sh'moh b'ah-hah-vah.

O Lord, open thou my lips, and my mouth shall declare thy
praise.
  Blessed art thou, O Lord our God and God of our fathers,
God of Abraham, God of Isaac, and God of Jacob, the great,
mighty and revered God, the most high God, who bestowest
lovingkindnesses, and possessest all things; who rememberest
the pious deeds of the patriarchs, and in love wilt bring a redeemer to their children's children for thy name's sake.

On the Sabbath of Repentance, say:

zahk-ray-noo lah-chaye-yeem mel-lech cha-fayts bah-chaye-yeem v'chaht-
vay-noo b'say-fer ha-chaye-yeem, l'mah-ahn-cha elo-heemchaye-yeem

Remember us unto life, O King, who delightest in life, and
inscribe us in the book of life, for thine own sake, O living God.

mel-ek oh-zayr oo-moh-shee-ah oo-mah-gayn, ba-rooch ah-tah ah-doh-
nye, mah-gayn ahv-rah-hahm. a-tah gee-bohr l'oh-lahm ah-doh-nye
m'chaye-yeh may-teem a-tah rahv l'hoh-shee-ah.

O King, Helper, Saviour and Shield. Blessed art thou, O
Lord, the Shield of Abraham.

Thou, O Lord, art mighty for ever, thou quickenest the
dead, thou art mighty to save.

From the Sabbath after Sh'mini Atsereth until the First Day
of Passover add:

mah-sheev ha-roo-ach oo-moh-reed   hahg-gah-shem

Thou causest the wind to blow and the rain to fall.

m'chal-kayl chaye-yeem b'cheh-sed m'chay-yay may-teem b'rah-chah-
meem rah-veem, soh-maych nohf-leem v'roh-fay choh-leem oo-mah-teer
ah-soo-reem oom-kah-yaym em-oo-nah-toh lee-shay-nay ah-fahr, mee
chah-moh-chah bah-ahl g'voo-roht oo-mee doh-meh lahch mel-ek may-
meet oom-chah-yet oo-mats-mee-ach yeshua

Thou sustainest the living with lovingkindness, quickenest
the dead with great mercy, supportest the falling, healest the
sick, loosest the bound, and keepest thy faith to them that
sleep in the dust. Who is like unto thee, Lord of mighty acts,
and who resembleth thee, O King, who killest and quickenest,
and causest salvation to spring forth?

THE AMIDAH

The Congregation will stand for the Amidah.

אֲדֹנָי שְׂפָתַי תִּפְתָּח וּפִי יַגִּיד תְּהִלָּתֶךָ:

בָּרוּךְ אַתָּה יְיָ אֱלֹהֵינוּ וֵאלֹהֵי אֲבוֹתֵינוּ אֱלֹהֵי
אַבְרָהָם אֱלֹהֵי יִצְחָק וֵאלֹהֵי יַעֲקֹב הָאֵל הַגָּדוֹל
הַגִּבּוֹר וְהַנּוֹרָא אֵל עֶלְיוֹן גּוֹמֵל חֲסָדִים טוֹבִים
וְקוֹנֵה הַכֹּל וְזוֹכֵר חַסְדֵי אָבוֹת וּמֵבִיא גוֹאֵל
לִבְנֵי בְנֵיהֶם לְמַעַן שְׁמוֹ בְּאַהֲבָה:

On the Sabbath of Repentance, say:

(זָכְרֵנוּ לְחַיִּים. מֶלֶךְ חָפֵץ בַּחַיִּים. וְכָתְבֵנוּ בְּסֵפֶר הַחַיִּים.
לְמַעַנְךָ אֱלֹהִים חַיִּים.)

מֶלֶךְ עוֹזֵר וּמוֹשִׁיעַ וּמָגֵן: בָּרוּךְ אַתָּה יְיָ מָגֵן אַבְרָהָם:
אַתָּה גִּבּוֹר לְעוֹלָם אֲדֹנָי מְחַיֵּה מֵתִים אַתָּה רַב לְהוֹשִׁיעַ:

*From the Sabbath after Sh'mini Atsereth until the First Day
of Passover add:*

(מַשִּׁיב הָרוּחַ וּמוֹרִיד הַגָּשֶׁם:)

מְכַלְכֵּל חַיִּים בְּחֶסֶד מְחַיֵּה מֵתִים בְּרַחֲמִים
רַבִּים סוֹמֵךְ נוֹפְלִים וְרוֹפֵא חוֹלִים וּמַתִּיר
אֲסוּרִים וּמְקַיֵּם אֱמוּנָתוֹ לִישֵׁנֵי עָפָר. מִי
כָמוֹךָ בַּעַל גְּבוּרוֹת וּמִי דוֹמֶה לָּךְ מֶלֶךְ
מֵמִית וּמְחַיֶּה וּמַצְמִיחַ יְשׁוּעָה:

On the Sabbath of Penitence add:

mee cha-moh-cha ahv hah-rah-chah-meem zoh-chayr y'tsoo-rahv lah-chaye- yeem b'rah-chah-meem

Who is like unto thee, Father of mercy, who in mercy rememberest thy creatures unto life?

v'neh-eh-mahn ah-tah l'ha-cha-yoht may-teem, bah-rooch ah-tah ah-doh-nye, m'cha-yay ha-may-teem. ah-tah kah-dohsh v'sheem-cha kah-dohsh ook-doh-sheem b'chahl yohm y'ha-lah-loo-cha seh-lah, bah-rooch ah-tah ah-doh-nye, hah-ayl ha-kah-dohsh.

Yea, faithful art thou to quicken the dead. Blessed art thou, O Lord, who quickenest the dead.

Thou art holy, and thy name is holy, and holy beings praise thee daily. (Selah.) Blessed art thou, O Lord, the holy God.

On the Sabbath of Penitence conclude the Blessing thus:

ha-mel-ech   ha-kah-dohsh

the holy King.

GENESIS 2:1-3

ah-tah kee-dahsh-tah et yohm hahsh-vee-ee leesh-meh-cha, tahch-leet mah-ah-say sha-mah-yeem vah-ah-rets, oo-vay-rahch-toh mee-kahl haye-yah-meem v'kee-dahsh-toh mee-kahl hahz-mah- neem, v'chayn cha-toov b'toh-rah-teh-cha. vaye-choo-loo ha-shah-may-yeem v'ha-ah-rets v'chal ts'vah-ahm. vaye-chahl elo-heem baye-yohm hahsh-vee-ee m'lahch-toh ah-sher ah-sah vaye-yeesh-boht baye-yohm hahsh-vee-ee mee-kahl m'lahch-toh ah-sher ah-sah. vaye-vah-rech elo-heem et yohm hahsh-vee-ee vaye-kah-desh oh-toh kee voh shah-vaht mee-kahl m'lahch-toh ah-sher bah-rah elo-heem lah-ah-soht.

Thou didst hallow the seventh day unto thy name, as the end of the creation of heaven and earth, thou didst bless it above all days, and didst hallow it above all seasons, and thus it is written in thy law:

And the heaven and the earth were finished and all their host. And on the seventh day God had finished his work which he had made. And God blessed the seventh day, and he hallowed it, because he rested thereon from all his work which God had created and made.

A PRAYER FOR THE SABBATH

elo-hay-noo vay-loh-hay ah-voh-tay-noo, r'tsay veem-noo-cha-tay-noo kahd-shay-noo b'meets-voh-tey-cha v'tayn chel-kay-noo b'toh-rah-teh-cha, sahb-ay-noo mee-too-veh-cha v'sahm-chay-noo bee-shoo-ah-teh-cha v'tah-her lee-bay-noo l'ahv-d'cha beh-eh-met, v'hahn-chee-lay-noo ah-doh-nye elo-hey-noo b'ah-ha-vah oov-rah-tsohn sha-baht kahd-sheh-cha, v'yah-noo-choo vah yees -rah-el m'kahd-shay sh'meh-cha, bah-rooch ah-tah ah-doh-nye, m'kah-desh hahsh-shah-baht.

Our God and God of our fathers, accept our rest; sanctify us by thy commandments, and grant our portion in thy law;

On the Sabbath of Penitence add:

(מִי כָמְוֹךָ אַב הָרַחֲמִים . זוֹכֵר יְצוּרָיו לַחַיִּים בְּרַחֲמִים :)

וְנֶאֱמָן אַתָּה לְהַחֲיוֹת מֵתִים : בָּרוּךְ אַתָּה יְיָ
מְחַיֵּה הַמֵּתִים :

אַתָּה קָדוֹשׁ וְשִׁמְךָ קָדוֹשׁ וּקְדוֹשִׁים בְּכָל־יוֹם
יְהַלְלוּךָ פֶּלָה: בָּרוּךְ אַתָּה יְיָ הָאֵל הַקָּדוֹשׁ:

On the Sabbath of Penitence conclude the Blessing thus:

(הַמֶּלֶךְ הַקָּדוֹשׁ :)

GENESIS 2:1-3

אַתָּה קִדַּשְׁתָּ אֶת־יוֹם הַשְּׁבִיעִי לִשְׁמֶךָ . תַּכְלִית
מַעֲשֵׂה שָׁמַיִם וָאָרֶץ . וּבֵרַכְתּוֹ מִכָּל־הַיָּמִים וְקִדַּשְׁתּוֹ
מִכָּל־הַזְּמַנִּים.וְכֵן כָּתוּב בְּתוֹרָתֶךָ :

וַיְכֻלּוּ הַשָּׁמַיִם וְהָאָרֶץ וְכָל־צְבָאָם : וַיְכַל
אֱלֹהִים בַּיּוֹם הַשְּׁבִיעִי מְלַאכְתּוֹ אֲשֶׁר עָשָׂה
וַיִּשְׁבֹּת בַּיּוֹם הַשְּׁבִיעִי מִכָּל מְלַאכְתּוֹ אֲשֶׁר
עָשָׂה: וַיְבָרֶךְ אֱלֹהִים אֶת יוֹם הַשְּׁבִיעִי
וַיְקַדֵּשׁ אֹתוֹ כִּי בוֹ שָׁבַת מִכָּל מְלַאכְתּוֹ
אֲשֶׁר בָּרָא אֱלֹהִים לַעֲשׂוֹת :

A PRAYER FOR THE SABBATH

אֱלֹהֵינוּ וֵאלֹהֵי אֲבוֹתֵינוּ . רְצֵה בִמְנוּחָתֵנוּ.קַדְּשֵׁנוּ
בְּמִצְוֹתֶיךָ וְתֵן חֶלְקֵנוּ בְּתוֹרָתֶךָ . שַׂבְּעֵנוּ מִטּוּבֶךָ
וְשַׂמְּחֵנוּ בִּישׁוּעָתֶךָ . וְטַהֵר לִבֵּנוּ לְעָבְדְּךָ בֶּאֱמֶת.
וְהַנְחִילֵנוּ יְיָ אֱלֹהֵינוּ בְּאַהֲבָה וּבְרָצוֹן שַׁבַּת קָדְשֶׁךָ
וְיָנוּחוּ בוֹ יִשְׂרָאֵל מְקַדְּשֵׁי שְׁמֶךָ: בָּרוּךְ אַתָּה יְיָ
מְקַדֵּשׁ הַשַּׁבָּת :

123

(A Prayer for the Sabbath continued)

satisfy us with thy goodness, and gladden us with thy salvation; purify our hearts to serve thee in truth; and in thy love and favor, O Lord our God, let us inherit thy holy Sabbath; and may Israel, who hallow thy name, rest thereon. Blessed art thou, O Lord, who hallowest the Sabbath.

r'tseh ah-doh-nye elo-hay-noo b'ahm-m'cha yees ra-el oo-veet-fee-lah-tahm, v'ha-shayv et ha-ah-voh-dah leed-veer bay-teh-chah, v'ee-shay yees -rah-el, oot-fee-lah-tahm b'ah-ha-vah t'kah-bel b'rah-tsohn, oot-hee l'rah-tsohn tah-meed ah-voh-daht yees -rah-el ah-meh-cha.

Accept, O Lord our God, thy people Israel and their prayer; restore the service to the oracle of thy house; receive in love and favor both the fire-offerings of Israel and their prayer; and may the service of thy people Israel be ever acceptable unto thee.

On the Sabbath coincident with the New Moon add:

elo-hey-noo vay-loh-hay ahv-voh-tay-noo, yah-ah-leh v'yah-voh v'yah-gee-ah l'yay-rah-eh v'rah-tseh v'yeesh-sha-mah v'yee-pah-kehd v'yee-zah-cher zeech-roh-neh-noo oo-feek-doh-neh-noo, v'zeech-rohn ahv-voh-tay-noo, v'zeech-rohn mah-shee-ach behn dah-veed ahv-deh-cha, v'zeech-rohn y'roo-sha-lye-eem eer kahd-sheh-cha, v'zeech-rohn kahl ahm-m'cha bayt yees -rah-el l'fah-neh-cha, leef-lay-tah l'toh-vah l-chayn ool-che-sed ool-rah-cha-meem l'chaye-yeem ool-sha-lohm b'yohm.

On New Moon say: *On Passover say:*   *On Tabernacles say:*
rohsh ha-choh-desh   chahg hahm-mah-tsoht   chahg ha-soo-koht

ha-zeh, zahch-ray-noo ah-doh-nye elo-hey-noo boh l'toh-vah oo-fahk-deh-noo voh leev-rah-chah v'ho-shee-ay-noo voh l'haye-yeem, oov-d'vahr yeshua v'ra-cha-meem choos v'cha-nay-noo v'rah-chem ah-lay-noo v'hoh-shee-eh-noo, kee eh-lay-cha ay-nay-noo, kee el mel-ech cha-noon v'rah-choom ah-tah.

On the Sabbath coincident with the New Moon add:

Our God and God of our fathers! May our remembrance rise, come and be accepted before thee, with the remembrance of our fathers, of Messiah the son of David thy servant, of Jerusalem thy holy city, and of all thy people the house of Israel, bringing deliverance and well-being, grace, lovingkindness and mercy, life and peace on this day of the

(On New Moon:) Be mindful of us on this day of the New Moon.

(On Passover:) On this Feast of Unleavened Bread.

(On Tabernacles:) On this Feast of Tabernacles.

Remember us, O Lord our God, thereon for our well-being; be mindful of us for blessing, and save us unto life; by thy promise of salvation and mercy, spare us and be gracious unto us; have mercy upon us and save us; for our eyes are bent upon thee, because thou art a gracious and merciful God and King.

רְצֵה יְיָ אֱלֹהֵינוּ בְּעַמְּךָ יִשְׂרָאֵל וּבִתְפִלָּתָם . וְהָשֵׁב
אֶת־הָעֲבוֹדָה לִדְבִיר בֵּיתֶךָ וְאִשֵּׁי יִשְׂרָאֵל. וּתְפִלָּתָם
בְּאַהֲבָה תְקַבֵּל בְּרָצוֹן וּתְהִי לְרָצוֹן תָּמִיד עֲבוֹדַת
יִשְׂרָאֵל עַמֶּךָ :

On the Sabbath coincident with the New Moon add:

אֱלֹהֵינוּ וֵאלֹהֵי אֲבוֹתֵינוּ יַעֲלֶה וְיָבֹא וְיַגִּיעַ וְיֵרָאֶה וְיֵרָצֶה
וְיִשָּׁמַע וְיִפָּקֵד וְיִזָּכֵר זִכְרוֹנֵנוּ וּפִקְדוֹנֵנוּ וְזִכְרוֹן אֲבוֹתֵינוּ
וְזִכְרוֹן מָשִׁיחַ בֶּן דָּוִד עַבְדֶּךָ. וְזִכְרוֹן יְרוּשָׁלַיִם עִיר
קָדְשֶׁךָ וְזִכְרוֹן כָּל עַמְּךָ בֵּית יִשְׂרָאֵל לְפָנֶיךָ. לִפְלֵיטָה
לְטוֹבָה לְחֵן וּלְחֶסֶד וּלְרַחֲמִים לְחַיִּים וּלְשָׁלוֹם בְּיוֹם

On Tabernacles say:	*On Passover say:*	*On New Moon say:*
חַג הַסֻּכּוֹת	חַג הַמַּצּוֹת	רֹאשׁ הַחֹדֶשׁ

הַזֶּה: זָכְרֵנוּ יְיָ אֱלֹהֵינוּ בּוֹ לְטוֹבָה. וּפָקְדֵנוּ בוֹ לִבְרָכָה.
וְהוֹשִׁיעֵנוּ בּוֹ לְחַיִּים. וּבִדְבַר יְשׁוּעָה וְרַחֲמִים חוּס וְחָנֵּנוּ.
וְרַחֵם עָלֵינוּ וְהוֹשִׁיעֵנוּ. כִּי אֵלֶיךָ עֵינֵינוּ. כִּי אֵל מֶלֶךְ חַנּוּן
וְרַחוּם אָתָּה:

125

v'teh-che-zay-noo ay-nay-noo b'shoov-cha l'tsee-yohn b'rah-cha-meem.
bah-rooch ah-tah ah-doh-nye ha-mah-cha-zeer sh'kee-nah-toh l'tsee-yohn.

And let our eyes behold thy return in mercy to Zion.
Blessed art thou, O Lord, who restorest thy divine presence
unto Zion.

moh-deem ah-nahch-noo lahch sha-ah-tah hoo ah-doh-nye elo-hey-noo
veh-loh-hay ahv-voh-tay-noo l'oh-lahm vah-ed, tsoor cha-yay-noo mah-
gen yeesh-eh-noo ah-tah hoo l'dohr vah-dohr, noh-deh l'cha oon-sah-per
t'hee-lah-teh-cha ahl chay-yay-noo hahm-m'soo-reem b'yah-deh-cha v'ahl
neesh-moh-tay-noo hahp-p'koo-doht lach, v'ahl nees-say-cha sheh-b'chahl
yohm eem-mah-noo v'ahl neef-l'oh-teh-cha v'tohv-voh-tay-cha sheb-
b'chahl et eh-rev vah-voh-ker v'tsah-ha-rah-yeem ha-tohv kee loh chah-
loo rah-chamay-cha, v'ham-rah-chem kee lo tahm-moo cha-sah-day-cha
may-oh-lahm kee-vee-noo lach.

We give thanks unto thee, for thou art the Lord our God
and the God of our fathers for ever and ever; thou art the
rock of our lives, the shield of our salvation through every
generation. We will give thanks unto thee and declare thy
praise for our lives which are committed unto thy hand, and
for our souls which are in thy charge, and for thy miracles,
which are daily with us, and for thy wonders and thy benefits
which are wrought at all times, evening, morn and noon. O
thou who art all-good, whose mercies fail not; thou, merciful
being, whose lovingkindnesses never cease, we have ever hoped
in thee.

v'ahl koo-lahm yeet-bah-rach v'yeet-roh-mahm sheem-cha mahl-keh-noo
tah-meed l'oh-lahm vah-ed.

For all these things thy name, O our King, shall be continually blessed and exalted for ever and ever.

On the Sabbath of Penitence add:

ooch-tohv l'chaye-yeem toh-veem kahl b'nay v'ree-teh-chah

O inscribe all the children of thy covenant for a happy life.

v'chohl ha-chaye-yeem yoh-doo-cha seh-lah, vee-hah-lah-loo et sheem-
chah beh-eh-met ha-el y'shoo-ah-tay-noo v'ez-rah-tay-noo seh-lah, bah-
rooch ah-tah ah-doh-nye, ha-tohv sheem-cha ool-cha nah-eh l'hoh-doht.

And everything that liveth shall give thanks unto thee for
ever, and shall praise thy name in truth, O God, our salvation
and our help. Blessed art thou, O Lord, whose name is all-good,
and unto whom it is becoming to give thanks.

sha-lom rahv ahl yees-rah-el ahm-cha tah-seem l'oh-lahm, kee ah-tah
hoo me-lech ah-dohn l'chahl ha-sha-lom, v'tohv b'ay-nay-cha l'vah-rech
et ahm-cha yees-rah-el b'chahl et oov-chahl sha-ah beesh-loh-meh-cha.

Grant abundant peace unto Israel thy people for ever; for
thou art the sovereign Lord of all peace; and may it be good
in thy sight to bless thy people Israel at all times and at every
hour with thy peace.

וְתֶחֱזֶינָה עֵינֵינוּ בְּשׁוּבְךָ לְצִיּוֹן בְּרַחֲמִים׃ בָּרוּךְ אַתָּה יְיָ הַמַּחֲזִיר שְׁכִינָתוֹ לְצִיּוֹן׃

מוֹדִים אֲנַחְנוּ לָךְ שָׁאַתָּה הוּא יְיָ אֱלֹהֵינוּ וֵאלֹהֵי אֲבוֹתֵינוּ לְעוֹלָם וָעֶד צוּר חַיֵּינוּ מָגֵן יִשְׁעֵנוּ. אַתָּה הוּא לְדוֹר וָדוֹר נוֹדֶה לְּךָ וּנְסַפֵּר תְּהִלָּתֶךָ עַל־חַיֵּינוּ הַמְּסוּרִים בְּיָדֶךָ וְעַל־ נִשְׁמוֹתֵינוּ הַפְּקוּדוֹת לָךְ. וְעַל־נִסֶּיךָ שֶׁבְּכָל־ יוֹם עִמָּנוּ וְעַל נִפְלְאוֹתֶיךָ וְטוֹבוֹתֶיךָ שֶׁבְּכָל־ עֵת־עֶרֶב וָבֹקֶר וְצָהֳרָיִם . הַטּוֹב כִּי לֹא־ כָלוּ רַחֲמֶיךָ וְהַמְרַחֵם כִּי לֹא־תַמּוּ חֲסָדֶיךָ מֵעוֹלָם קִוִּינוּ לָךְ׃

וְעַל כֻּלָּם יִתְבָּרַךְ וְיִתְרוֹמַם שִׁמְךָ מַלְכֵּנוּ תָּמִיד לְעוֹלָם וָעֶד׃

On the Sabbath of Penitence add:

(וּכְתוֹב לְחַיִּים טוֹבִים כָּל־בְּנֵי־בְרִיתֶךָ ׃)

וְכֹל הַחַיִּים יוֹדוּךָ סֶּלָה וִיהַלְלוּ אֶת שִׁמְךָ בֶּאֱמֶת הָאֵל יְשׁוּעָתֵנוּ וְעֶזְרָתֵנוּ סֶלָה. בָּרוּךְ אַתָּה יְיָ הַטּוֹב שִׁמְךָ וּלְךָ נָאֶה לְהוֹדוֹת׃

שָׁלוֹם רָב עַל־יִשְׂרָאֵל עַמְּךָ תָּשִׂים לְעוֹלָם כִּי אַתָּה הוּא מֶלֶךְ אָדוֹן לְכָל הַשָּׁלוֹם. וְטוֹב בְּעֵינֶיךָ לְבָרֵךְ אֶת־עַמְּךָ יִשְׂרָאֵל בְּכָל־עֵת וּבְכָל־שָׁעָה בִּשְׁלוֹמֶךָ ׃

127

On the Sabbath of Penitence add:

b'seh-fer chaye-yeem b'rah-cha v'sha-lom oo-fahr-nah-sah toh-vah nee-zah-cher v'nee-kah-tehv l'fah-nay-cha ah-nach-noo v'chahl ahm-cha bayt yees-rah-el l'chaye-yeem toh-veem ool-sha-lom, bah-rooch a-tah ah-doh-nye oh-seh ha-sha-lom

In the book of life, blessing, peace and good sustenance may we be remembered and inscribed before thee, we and all thy people the house of Israel, for a happy life and for peace. Blessed art thou, O Lord, who makest peace.

bah-rooch ah-tah ah-doh-nye ham-va-rech et ah-moh yees-rah-el bah-sha-lom

Blessed art thou, O Lord, who blessest thy people Israel with peace.

elo-hye, n'tsohr l'sho-nee meh-rah, oo-s'fah-tye mee-dah-behr meer-mah, v'leem-kah-l'lye naf-shee tee-dohm, v'naf-shee keh-ah-fahr lah-kohl tee-yeh. p'tach lee-bee b'toh-rah-teh-chah, oo'v'mee-tsvoh-teh-chah tir-dohf nahf-shee. v'chol ha-choh-shveem ah-lye rah-ah, m'hey-rah hah-fer ah-tsah-tahm v'kahl-kel mah-cha-shahv'tahm. ah-seh l'mah-ahn sh-meh-chah, ah-seh l'mah-ahn y'mee-neh-chah ah-seh l'mah-ahn k'doo-shah-teh-chah, ah-seh l'mah-ahn toh-rah-teh-chah. l'mah-ahn yeh-chal-tsoon v'dee-deh-chah hoh-she-ah   y'meen-chah vah-ah-neh-nee.

O my God! Guard my tongue from evil and my lips from speaking guile; and to such as curse me let my soul be dumb, yea, let my soul be unto all as the dust. Open my heart to thy law, and let my soul pursue thy commandments. If any design evil against me, speedily make their counsel of none effect, and frustrate their designs. Do it for the sake of thy name, do it for the sake of thy right hand, do it for the sake of thy holiness, do it for the sake of thy law. In order that thy beloved ones may be delivered, O save with thy right hand, and answer me.

yee-yoo l'rah-tsohn eem-ray fee v'heg-yohn lee-bee l'fah-neh-chah, ah-doh-nye tsoo-ree v'go-ah-lee. oh-seh sha-lohm bee-m-roh-mahv, hoo yah-ah-seh sha-lohm ah-ley-noo v'ahl kol yees-ra-el v'eem-roo a-men.

Let the words of my mouth and the meditation of my heart be acceptable before thee, O Lord, my Rock and my Redeemer. He who maketh peace in his high places, may he make peace for us and for all Israel, and say ye, Amen.

On the Sabbath of Penitence add:

(בְּסֵפֶר חַיִּים בְּרָכָה וְשָׁלוֹם וּפַרְנָסָה טוֹבָה נִזָּכֵר וְנִכָּתֵב
לְפָנֶיךָ אֲנַחְנוּ וְכָל־עַמְּךָ בֵּית יִשְׂרָאֵל לְחַיִּים טוֹבִים וּלְשָׁלוֹם:
בָּרוּךְ אַתָּה יְיָ עוֹשֵׂה הַשָּׁלוֹם:)

בָּרוּךְ אַתָּה יְיָ הַמְבָרֵךְ אֶת־עַמּוֹ יִשְׂרָאֵל בַּשָּׁלוֹם:

אֱלֹהַי. נְצוֹר לְשׁוֹנִי מֵרָע וּשְׂפָתַי מִדַּבֵּר מִרְמָה
וְלִמְקַלְלַי נַפְשִׁי תִדוֹם וְנַפְשִׁי כֶּעָפָר לַכֹּל תִּהְיֶה: פְּתַח
לִבִּי בְּתוֹרָתֶךָ וּבְמִצְוֹתֶיךָ תִּרְדּוֹף נַפְשִׁי וְכֹל הַחוֹשְׁבִים
עָלַי רָעָה מְהֵרָה הָפֵר עֲצָתָם וְקַלְקֵל מַחֲשַׁבְתָּם.
עֲשֵׂה לְמַעַן שְׁמֶךָ. עֲשֵׂה לְמַעַן יְמִינֶךָ. עֲשֵׂה לְמַעַן
קְדֻשָּׁתֶךָ. עֲשֵׂה לְמַעַן תּוֹרָתֶךָ. לְמַעַן יֵחָלְצוּן יְדִידֶיךָ
הוֹשִׁיעָה יְמִינְךָ וַעֲנֵנִי: יִהְיוּ לְרָצוֹן אִמְרֵי פִי וְהֶגְיוֹן
לִבִּי לְפָנֶיךָ יְיָ צוּרִי וְגֹאֲלִי: עֹשֶׂה שָׁלוֹם בִּמְרוֹמָיו
הוּא יַעֲשֶׂה שָׁלוֹם עָלֵינוּ וְעַל כָּל יִשְׂרָאֵל וְאִמְרוּ אָמֵן:

y'hee rah-tsohn meel-fah-neh-chah, ah-doh-nye eh-loh-hey-noo veh-loh-hey ah-voh-tey-noo, sheh-yee-bah-neh bayt ha-meek-dash beem-hey-rah v'yah-mey-noo, v'ten chel-key-noo b'toh-rah-teh-chah. v'shahm nah-ah-vahd-chah b'yeer-ah, kee-may oh-lahm oo-che-sha-neem, kahd-moh-nee-yot v'ahr-vah lah-doh-nye meen-chaht y'hoo-dah vee-y'roo-sha-lyeim kee-may oh-lahm oo-ch'sha-neem kaḥd-moh-nee-yoht.

May it be thy will, O Lord our God and God of our fathers, that the temple be speedily rebuilt in our days, and grant our portion in thy law. And there we will serve thee with awe, as in the days of old, and as in ancient years. Then shall the offering of Judah and Jerusalem be pleasant unto the Lord, as in the days of old, and as in ancient years.

TORAH READING

HAF-TORAH READING

SERMON

MOURNER'S KADDISH

yeet-gah-dahl v'yeet-kah-dahsh sh'may rah-bah b'ahl-mah dee v'rah cheer-oo-tay v'yahm-leek mal-choo-tay b'chah-yay-chohn oov-yoh-may-chohn. oov-chay-yay d'chahl bayt yees-rah-el. ba-ah-gah-lah oo-veez-mahn kah-reev v'eem-roo. ah-mayn. y'hay sh'may rah-bah m'vah-rahch l'ah-lahm ool-ahl-may ahl-may-yah. yeet-bah-rahch v'yeesh-tah-bach v'yeet-pah-ahr v'yeet-roh-mahm. v'yeet-nah-say v'yeet-ha-dahr v'yeet-ah-leh v'yeet-ha-lahl sh'may d'kood-shah b'reech hoo l'ay-lah meen kol beer-cha-tah v'shee-rah-tah. toosh-b'cha-tah v'neh-che-mah-tah dah-ah-mee-rahn b'ahl-mah v'eem-roo, ah-mayn. y'hey sh'lah-mah rah-bah meen sh'mah-yah v'chey-yeem ah-lay-noo v'ahl kol yees-rah-el v'eem-roo. ah-mayn. oh-sheh sha-lohm beem-roh-mahv hoo yah-ah-seh sha-lohm ah-lay-noo v'ahl kol yees-rah-el v'eem-roo. ah-mayn.

Mourner: Magnified and sanctified be his great name in the world which he hath created according to his will. May he establish his kingdom in your lifetime and in your days, and in the lifetime of all the house of Israel, speedily and at a near time; and say ye, Amen.

Cong. and Mourner: Let his great name be blessed for ever and ever.

Mourner: Blessed, praised and glorified, exalted, extolled and honored, adored and lauded, be the name of the Holy One, blessed be he, beyond, yea, beyond all blessings and hymns, praises and songs, which are uttered in the world; and say ye, Amen.

May there be abundant peace from heaven, and life for us and for all Israel; and say ye, Amen.

May he who maketh peace in his high places, make peace for us and for all Israel; and say ye, Amen.

130

יְהִי רָצוֹן מִלְּפָנֶיךָ יְיָ אֱלֹהֵינוּ וֵאלֹהֵי אֲבוֹתֵינוּ שֶׁיִּבָּנֶה
בֵּית הַמִּקְדָּשׁ בִּמְהֵרָה בְיָמֵינוּ וְתֵן חֶלְקֵנוּ בְּתוֹרָתֶךָ :
וְשָׁם נַעֲבָדְךָ בְּיִרְאָה כִּימֵי עוֹלָם וּכְשָׁנִים קַדְמוֹנִיּוֹת:
וְעָרְבָה לַיָי מִנְחַת יְהוּדָה וִירוּשָׁלֶַים כִּימֵי עוֹלָם
וּכְשָׁנִים קַדְמוֹנִיּוֹת :

MOURNER'S KADDISH

Mourner:

יִתְגַּדַּל וְיִתְקַדַּשׁ שְׁמֵהּ רַבָּא, בְּעָלְמָא דִי־בְרָא
כִרְעוּתֵהּ.וְיַמְלִיךְ מַלְכוּתֵהּ. בְּחַיֵּיכוֹן וּבְיוֹמֵיכוֹן,וּבְחַיֵּי
דְכָל בֵּית־יִשְׂרָאֵל. בַּעֲגָלָא וּבִזְמַן קָרִיב וְאִמְרוּ. אָמֵן:

Cong. and Mourner:

יְהֵא שְׁמֵהּ רַבָּא, מְבָרַךְ לְעָלַם וּלְעָלְמֵי עָלְמַיָּא:

Mourner:

יִתְבָּרַךְ וְיִשְׁתַּבַּח, וְיִתְפָּאַר וְיִתְרוֹמַם, וְיִתְנַשֵּׂא
וְיִתְהַדָּר, וְיִתְעַלֶּה וְיִתְהַלָּל שְׁמֵהּ דְקֻדְשָׁא,   בְּרִיךְ
הוּא.   לְעֵלָּא   מִן־כָּל־בִּרְכָתָא וְשִׁירָתָא,
תֻּשְׁבְּחָתָא וְנֶחֱמָתָא, דַּאֲמִירָן בְּעָלְמָא. וְאִמְרוּ. אָמֵן:

יְהֵא שְׁלָמָא רַבָּא מִן שְׁמַיָּא, וְחַיִּים עָלֵינוּ,
וְעַל כָּל יִשְׂרָאֵל, וְאִמְרוּ. אָמֵן:
עֹשֶׂה שָׁלוֹם בִּמְרוֹמָיו, הוּא יַעֲשֶׂה שָׁלוֹם, עָלֵינוּ,
וְעַל כָּל יִשְׂרָאֵל, וְאִמְרוּ. אָמֵן:

131

THE LORD'S PRAYER

ah-vee-noo sheh-bah-shah-mye-eem yeet-kah-dash sh'meh-chah tah-voh
mahl-choo-teh-chah yeh-ah-seh r'tzohn'chah k'moh vah-shah-mye-eem
ken bah-ah-retz. et lechem choo-keh-noo ten lah-noo hah-yohm oo-
s'lach lah-noo et choh-voh-tey-noo kah-ah-sher sah-lach-noo gahm ah-
nach-noo l'chah-yah-vey-noo. v'ahl t'vee-ey-noo lee-day nee-sah-yohn
kee eem chal-tsey-noo meen hah-rah kee l'chah hah-mahm-la-chah
v'hah-g'voo-rah v'hah-teef-eh-ret l'ol-mey oh-lah-meem ah-meyn.

Our Father which art in heaven, hallowed be thy name. Thy
kingdom come. Thy will be done in earth, as it is in heaven.
Give us this day our daily bread. And forgive us our debts, as
we forgive our debtors. And lead us not into temptation, but
deliver us from evil: for thine is the kingdom, and the power,
and the glory, for ever. Amen.

AHLEYNOO

ah-lay-noo l'shah-beh-ach lah-ah-dohn ha-kohl lah-tayt g'doo-lah l'yoh-
tser b'ray-sheet sheh-loh ah-sah-noo k'goh-yay ha-ah-ra-tsoht v'loh
sah-mah-noo k'meesh-p'choht ha-ah-dah-mah shel-loh sahm chel-kee-noo
kah-hem v'goh-rah-lay-noo k'chahl ha-moh-nahm. vah-ah-nach-noo kohr-
eem oo-meesh-tah-chah-veem oom-oh-deem leef-nay me-lech mal-chay
hahm-lah-cheem ha-kah-dohsh bah-rooch hoo sheh-hoo noh-teh shah-
mye-eem v'yoh-sayd ah-retz oo-moh-shahv y'kah-roh bah-shah-mye-eem
mee-mah-ahl oosh-chee-naht oo-zoh b'gahv-hey m'roh-meem. hoo elo-
hey-noo ayn ohd. eh-met mal-kay-noo eh-fes zoo-lah-toh. kah-kah-toov
b'toh-rah-toh v'yah-dah-tah ha-yohm vah-ha-shayv-tah el l'vah-veh-cha
kee ah-doh-nye hoo ha-loh-heem bahsh-sha-mye-eem mee-mah-ahl v'ahl
ha-ah-rets mee-tah-chaht ayn ohd.

It is our duty to praise the Lord of all things, to ascribe
greatness to him who formed the world in the beginning, since
he hath not made us like the nations of other lands, and hath
not placed us like other families of the earth, since he hath not
assigned unto us a portion as unto them, nor a lot as unto all
their multitude.

For we bend the knee and offer worship and thanks before
the supreme King of kings, the Holy One, blessed be he.

Who stretched forth the heavens and laid the foundations of
the earth, the seat of whose glory is in the heavens above, and
the abode of whose might is in the loftiest heights. He is our
God; there is none else: in truth he is our King; there is none
besides him; as it is written in his law, and thou shalt know
this day, and lay it to thine heart, that the Lord he is God in
heaven above and upon the earth beneath; there is none else.

THE LORD'S PRAYER

אָבִינוּ שֶׁבַּשָּׁמַיִם יִתְקַדַּשׁ שְׁמֶךָ: תָּבֹא
מַלְכוּתֶךָ יֵעָשֶׂה רְצוֹנְךָ כְּמוֹ בַשָּׁמַיִם
כֵּן בָּאָרֶץ: אֶת־לֶחֶם חֻקֵּנוּ תֶּן־ לָנוּ
הַיּוֹם: וּסְלַח־לָנוּ אֶת־חוֹבוֹתֵינוּ כַּאֲשֶׁר
סָלַחְנוּ גַם־ אֲנַחְנוּ לְחַיָּבֵינוּ: וְאַל־
תְּבִיאֵנוּ לִידֵי נִסָּיוֹן כִּי אִם־ חַלְּצֵנוּ
מִן־הָרָע כִּי לְךָ הַמַּמְלָכָה וְהַגְּבוּרָה
וְהַתִּפְאֶרֶת לְעוֹלְמֵי עוֹלָמִים אָמֵן:

AHLEYNOO

עָלֵינוּ לְשַׁבֵּחַ לַאֲדוֹן הַכֹּל לָתֵת גְּדֻלָּה לְיוֹצֵר
בְּרֵאשִׁית שֶׁלֹּא עָשָׂנוּ כְּגוֹיֵי הָאֲרָצוֹת וְלֹא שָׂמָנוּ
כְּמִשְׁפְּחוֹת הָאֲדָמָה שֶׁלֹּא שָׂם חֶלְקֵנוּ כָּהֶם וְגֹרָלֵנוּ
כְּכָל־הֲמוֹנָם:
וַאֲנַחְנוּ כּוֹרְעִים וּמִשְׁתַּחֲוִים וּמוֹדִים לִפְנֵי מֶלֶךְ
מַלְכֵי הַמְּלָכִים הַקָּדוֹשׁ בָּרוּךְ הוּא.
שֶׁהוּא נוֹטֶה שָׁמַיִם וְיוֹסֵד אָרֶץ וּמוֹשַׁב יְקָרוֹ בַּשָּׁמַיִם
מִמַּעַל וּשְׁכִינַת עֻזּוֹ בְּגָבְהֵי מְרוֹמִים: הוּא אֱלֹהֵינוּ אֵין
עוֹד. אֱמֶת מַלְכֵּנוּ אֶפֶס זוּלָתוֹ. כַּכָּתוּב בְּתוֹרָתוֹ
וְיָדַעְתָּ הַיּוֹם וַהֲשֵׁבֹתָ אֶל־לְבָבֶךָ כִּי יְיָ הוּא הָאֱלֹהִים
בַּשָּׁמַיִם מִמַּעַל וְעַל־הָאָרֶץ מִתָּחַת אֵין עוֹד:

WE THEREFORE HOPE IN THEE

ahl kayn nahk-veh l'cha ah-doh-nye elo-hay-noo leer-oht m'hay-rah
b'teef-eh-ret oo-zeh-cha l'ha-ah-veer geel-loo-leem meen ha-ah-rets v'ha-
eh-lee-leem kah-roht yee-kah-ray-toon. l'tah-kayn oh-lahm b'mahl-choot
shah-dye v'chol b'nay vah-sahr yeek-r'oo veesh-meh-chah. l'hahf-noht
ay-leh-cha kahl reesh-ay ah-rets. yah-kee-roo v'yeed-oo kahl yohsh-vay
tay-vayl kee l'chah teech-rah kahl beh-rech tee-shah-vah kahl lah-shohn.
l'fah-neh-cha ah-doh-nye elo-hey-noo yeech-r'oo v'yeep-poh-loo. v'leech-
vohd sheem-cha y'kahr yee-tay-noo. vee-yahk-b'loo choo-lahm et ohl
mahl-choo-teh-cha. v'teem-lohch ah-lay-hem m'hay-rah l'oh-lahm vah-ed.
kee hahm-mahl-choot shel-cha hee ool-ohl-may ahd teem-lohk b'cha-
vohd. kah-ka-toov b'toh-rah-teh-cha ah-doh-nye yeem-lohk l'oh-lahm
vah-ed. v'neh-eh-mahr v'hye-yah ah-doh-nye l'meh-lech ahl kahl ha-ah-
rets. bah-yohm ha-hoo yee-yeh ah-doh-nye eh-chahd oosh-moh eh-chahd.

We therefore hope in thee, O Lord our God, that we may speedily behold the glory of thy might, when thou wilt remove the abominations from the earth, and the idols will be utterly cut off, when the world will be perfected under the kingdom of the Almighty, and all the children of flesh will call upon thy name, when thou wilt turn unto thyself all the wicked of the earth. Let all the inhabitants of the world perceive and know that unto thee every knee must bend, every tongue must swear. Before thee, O Lord our God, let them bow and fall; and unto thy glorious name let them give honor; let them all accept the yoke of thy kingdom, and do thou reign over them speedily, and for ever and ever. For the kingdom is thine, and to all eternity thou wilt reign in glory; as it is written in thy law, the Lord shall reign for ever and ever. And it is said, and the Lord shall be king over all the earth; on that day shall the Lord be One, and his name One.

KIDDUSH

bah-rooch ah-tah ah-doh-nye elo-hey-noo meh-lech ha-oh-lahm boh-ray
p'ree ha-gah-fen. bah-rooch ah-tah ah-doh-nye elo-hey-noo meh-lech ha-
oh-lahm ah-sher keed-sha-noo b'meets-voh-tahv v'rah-tsah vah-noo v'shah-
baht kahd-shoh b'ah-ha-vah oov-rahts-ohn heen-chee-lah-noo zee-kah-
rohn l'mah-ah-seh v'ray-sheet, kee hoo yohm t'chee-lah l'mik-ray-ay
koh-desh zay-cher lee-tsee-aht meetz-rah-yeem. kee vah-noo vah-chahr-
tah v'oh-tah-noo kee-dahsh-tah me-kohl ha-ah-meem v'sha-baht kahd-
sh'cha b'ah-ha-vah oov-rah-tsohn heen-chahl-tah-noo. bah-rooch ah-tah
ah-doh-nye m'kah-desh ha-sha-baht.

Blessed art thou, O Lord our God, King of the universe, who createst the fruit of the vine.

Blessed art thou, O Lord our God, King of the universe, who hast sanctified us by thy commandments and hast taken pleasure in us, and in love and favor hast given us the holy Sabbath as an inheritance, a memorial of the creation — that day also being the first of the holy convocations, in remembrance of the departure from Egypt. For thou hast chosen us

WE THEREFORE HOPE IN THEE

עַל־כֵּן נְקַוֶּה לְךָ יְיָ אֱלֹהֵינוּ לִרְאוֹת מְהֵרָה בְּתִפְאֶרֶת
עֻזֶּךָ לְהַעֲבִיר גִּלּוּלִים מִן הָאָרֶץ וְהָאֱלִילִים כָּרוֹת
יִכָּרֵתוּן ۰ לְתַקֵּן עוֹלָם בְּמַלְכוּת שַׁדַּי וְכָל־בְּנֵי בָשָׂר
יִקְרְאוּ בִשְׁמֶךָ ۰ לְהַפְנוֹת אֵלֶיךָ כָּל־רִשְׁעֵי אָרֶץ ۰ יַכִּירוּ
וְיֵדְעוּ כָּל־יוֹשְׁבֵי תֵבֵל כִּי לְךָ תִּכְרַע־כָּל־בֶּרֶךְ תִּשָּׁבַע
כָּל־לָשׁוֹן: לְפָנֶיךָ יְיָ אֱלֹהֵינוּ יִכְרְעוּ וְיִפּוֹלוּ ۰ וְלִכְבוֹד
שִׁמְךָ יְקָר יִתֵּנוּ ۰ וִיקַבְּלוּ כֻלָּם אֶת־עוֹל מַלְכוּתֶךָ ۰
וְתִמְלוֹךְ עֲלֵיהֶם מְהֵרָה לְעוֹלָם וָעֶד ۰ כִּי הַמַּלְכוּת שֶׁלְּךָ
הִיא וּלְעוֹלְמֵי עַד תִּמְלוֹךְ בְּכָבוֹד: כַּכָּתוּב בְּתוֹרָתֶךָ
יְיָ יִמְלֹךְ לְעֹלָם וָעֶד: וְנֶאֱמַר וְהָיָה יְיָ לְמֶלֶךְ עַל
כָּל־הָאָרֶץ ۰ בַּיּוֹם הַהוּא יִהְיֶה יְיָ אֶחָד וּשְׁמוֹ אֶחָד:

KIDDUSH

בָּרוּךְ אַתָּה יְיָ אֱלֹהֵינוּ מֶלֶךְ הָעוֹלָם בּוֹרֵא פְּרִי הַגָּפֶן:

בָּרוּךְ אַתָּה יְיָ אֱלֹהֵינוּ מֶלֶךְ הָעוֹלָם אֲשֶׁר קִדְּשָׁנוּ
בְּמִצְוֹתָיו וְרָצָה בָנוּ וְשַׁבַּת קָדְשׁוֹ בְּאַהֲבָה וּבְרָצוֹן
הִנְחִילָנוּ זִכָּרוֹן לְמַעֲשֵׂה בְרֵאשִׁית ۰ כִּי הוּא יוֹם תְּחִלָּה
לְמִקְרָאֵי קֹדֶשׁ זֵכֶר לִיצִיאַת מִצְרָיִם ۰ כִּי־בָנוּ בָחַרְתָּ
וְאוֹתָנוּ קִדַּשְׁתָּ מִכָּל־הָעַמִּים וְשַׁבַּת קָדְשְׁךָ בְּאַהֲבָה
וּבְרָצוֹן הִנְחַלְתָּנוּ: בָּרוּךְ אַתָּה יְיָ מְקַדֵּשׁ הַשַּׁבָּת:

(Kiddush continued)

and sanctified us above all nations, and in love and favor hast given us the holy Sabbath as an inheritance. Blessed art thou, O Lord, who hallowest the Sabbath.

THERE IS NONE LIKE OUR GOD

ayn keh-loh-hay-noo, ayn kah-doh-nay-noo ayn k'mahl-kay-noo, ayn k'moh-shee-aye-noo. mee che-loh-hay-noo, mee chah-doh-nay-noo mee ch'mahl-kay-noo, mee ch'moh-she-aye-noo noh-deh leh-loh-hay-noo, noh-deh lah-doh-nay-noo noh-deh l'mahl-kay-noo, noh-deh l'moh-shee-aye-noo ba-rooch elo-hay-noo, ba-rooch ah-doh-nye-noo ba-rooch mal-kay-noo, ba-rooch moh-shee-aye-noo ah-tah hoo elo-hay-noo ah-tah hoo ah-doh-nay-noo ah-tah hoo mahl-kay-noo ah-tah hoo moh-shee-aye-noo ah-tah hoo she-heek-tee-roo, ah-voh-tay-noo l'fah-neh-cha et k'toh-ret ha-sah-meem.

There is none like our God, none like our Lord, none like our King, none like our Saviour. Who is like our God, who like our King, who like our Saviour? We will give thanks unto our God, we will give thanks unto our Lord, we will give thanks unto our King, we will give thanks unto our Saviour. Blessed be our God, blessed be our Lord, blessed be our King, blessed be our Saviour. Thou art our God, thou art our Lord, thou art our King, thou art our Saviour. Thou art one unto whom our fathers burnt the incense of spices.

ADON OLOM

ah-dohn oh-lahm ah-sher mal-lach b'teh-rehm kohl y'tseer neev-rah. l'et nah-ah-sah v'chef-tsoh kohl. ah-zay me-lech sh'moh neek-rah. v'ah-chah-ray keech-loht ha-kohl. l'vah-doh yeem-lohch noh-rah. v'hoo ha-yah v'hoo hoh-veh. v'hoo yee-yeh b'teef-ah-rah. v'hoo eh-chad v'ayn shay-nee l'hahm-shel loh l'hach-bee-rah. b'lee ray-sheet b'lee tach-leet. v'loh ha-ohz v'hahm-mees-rah. v'hoo ay-lee v'chye goh-ah-lee. v'tsoor chehv-lee b'ayt tsah-rah. v'hoo nee-see oo-mah-nohs lee. m'naht koh-see b'yohm ehk-rah. b'yah-doh ahf-keed roo-chee. b'ayt ee-shahn v'ah-ee-rah. v'eem roo-chee g'vee-yah-tee. ah-doh-nye lee v'loh ee-rah.

He is Lord of the universe, who reigned ere any creature yet was formed:

At the time when all things were made by his desire, then was his name proclaimed King.

And after all things shall have had an end, he alone, the dreaded one, shall reign;

Who was, who is, and who will be in glory.

And he is One, and there is no second to compare to him, to consort with him:

Without beginning, without end: to him belong strength and dominion.

THERE IS NONE LIKE OUR GOD

אֵין כֵּאלֹהֵינוּ . אֵין כַּאדוֹנֵינוּ . אֵין כְּמַלְכֵּנוּ . אֵין
כְּמוֹשִׁיעֵנוּ : מִי כֵאלֹהֵינוּ . מִי כַאדוֹנֵינוּ . מִי כְמַלְכֵּנוּ ,
מִי כְמוֹשִׁיעֵנוּ : נוֹדֶה לֵאלֹהֵינוּ . נוֹדֶה לַאדוֹנֵינוּ . נוֹדֶה
לְמַלְכֵּנוּ . נוֹדֶה לְמוֹשִׁיעֵנוּ : בָּרוּךְ אֱלֹהֵינוּ . בָּרוּךְ
אֲדוֹנֵינוּ . בָּרוּךְ מַלְכֵּנוּ . בָּרוּךְ מוֹשִׁיעֵנוּ : אַתָּה הוּא
אֱלֹהֵינוּ . אַתָּה הוּא אֲדוֹנֵינוּ . אַתָּה הוּא מַלְכֵּנוּ . אַתָּה
הוּא מוֹשִׁיעֵנוּ . אַתָּה הוּא שֶׁהִקְטִירוּ אֲבוֹתֵינוּ לְפָנֶיךָ
אֶת קְטֹרֶת הַסַּמִּים :

ADON OLOM

אֲדוֹן עוֹלָם אֲשֶׁר מָלַךְ . בְּטֶרֶם כָּל־יְצִיר
נִבְרָא : לְעֵת נַעֲשָׂה בְחֶפְצוֹ כֹּל . אֲזַי מֶלֶךְ
שְׁמוֹ נִקְרָא : וְאַחֲרֵי כִּכְלוֹת הַכֹּל . לְבַדּוֹ
יִמְלוֹךְ נוֹרָא : וְהוּא הָיָה וְהוּא הֹוֶה . וְהוּא
יִהְיֶה בְּתִפְאָרָה : וְהוּא אֶחָד וְאֵין שֵׁנִי .
לְהַמְשִׁיל לוֹ לְהַחְבִּירָה : בְּלִי רֵאשִׁית בְּלִי
תַכְלִית . וְלוֹ הָעֹז וְהַמִּשְׂרָה . וְהוּא אֵלִי וְחַי
גֹּאֲלִי . וְצוּר חֶבְלִי בְּעֵת צָרָה : וְהוּא נִסִּי

יְמָנֹס לִי . מְנָת כּוֹסִי בְּיוֹם אֶקְרָא : בְּיָדוֹ
אַפְקִיד רוּחִי . בְּעֵת אִישָׁן וְאָעִירָה : וְעִם־
רוּחִי גְּוִיָּתִי . יְיָ לִי וְלֹא אִירָא :

(Adon Olom continued)

And he is my God — my Redeemer liveth — and a rock in my travail in time of distress:

And he is my banner and my refuge, the portion of my cup on the day when I call.

Into his hand I commend my spirit, when I sleep and when I wake;

And with my spirit, my body also: the Lord is with me, and I will not fear.

BENEDICTION

NUMBERS 6:24-26

y'vah-reh-ch'chah ah-doh-nye v'yeesh-m'reh-chah. yah-ehr ah-doh-nye pah-nahv eh-leh-chah vee-choo-neh-chah. ye-sah ah-doh-nye pah-nahv eh-leh-chah v'yah-seym l'chah sha-lom.

The Lord bless thee, and keep thee: the Lord make his face shine upon thee, and be gracious unto thee: the Lord lift up his countenance upon thee, and give thee peace.

BENEDICTION
NUMBERS 6:24-26

יְבָרֶכְךָ יְהוָֹה וְיִשְׁמְרֶךָ׃   יָאֵר יְהוָֹה
פָּנָיו אֵלֶיךָ וִיחֻנֶּךָ׃   יִשָּׂא יְהוָֹה פָּנָיו
אֵלֶיךָ וְיָשֵׂם לְךָ שָׁלוֹם׃

Appendixes

AN EFFECTIVE JEWISH HOME BIBLE STUDY

Imagine, if you will, a Jewish family who believe in Yeshua and open their door to anyone who would like to come one night a week to a home Torah study. As you walk into the door of their home, you notice yahmakahs lying next to a guest book. You put on a yahmakah, perhaps, and sign the guest book, providing your address, zip code and phone number.

You walk past the Jewish pastries prepared and covered in the dining room where refreshments will be served after the Torah study. Before long someone has given you a Bible and a song sheet of Jewish music, and you soon find yourself clapping rhythmically to the Jewish songs, some traditional, some based on a Hebrew New Testament, but all led by a musician whose testimony in word and song has "Jewish soul."

The Torah teacher puts you at ease with Jewish humor and Yiddish bon-mots and stirs your interest with exciting announcements of up-coming special events at this Torah study. Next week there will be a film on Israel, the following week there will be an Israeli singer who will share how God has miraculously touched her life. The week after that a Jewish ex-drug addict will tell his breath-taking story. You get the impression that there is so much going on in this Jewish home that you're going to miss out on all the action if you're not here every week, bringing your friends and family.

Next there is an informal get-acquainted time in which each person stands to give his name, where he's from and is given the opportunity to share a word or two, perhaps, on what he's especially thankful for or glad about tonight. Answers to prayer and testimonies and smiles soon begin to crackle all around the room.

The Torah teacher then asks someone in the audience to share her testimony, and for 10-15 minutes you hear how it happened that another Jewish person came to believe in Yeshua and still remained Jewish in the process! Her humorous and yet touching story strangely stirs you, so that afterwards when you sing the shema, you experience a strange new warmth in the room.

The Torah teacher obviously knows the Bible. He comments on the Hebrew and relates the Torah to the prophets and the New Testament, pointing to the Messianic prophecies that predict the coming of Yeshua. The Torah teacher is obviously a likeable man with easy-going humor, yet you can also see that he is a man with great love for and dedication to the Jewish people. For example, you know that he has gone to great trouble to drive many people to this home in his own car. His whole attitude is that of a servant and not a knacker (big shot). You notice that he seems to derive great peace from the Word of God, and his teaching has practical application for healthy day-to-day peaceful living.

At the close of his thirty minute teaching from the Torah and the prophets, he asks you to bow your head along with everyone else and pray a prayer in unison with them in which you all promise the God of Israel that if he will show you Yeshua is for real, then you will obey him. The Torah teacher asks all those who would appreciate prayer concerning this matter to raise their hands. (When those who are searching are identified, they can be prayed with later privately.) The Torah teacher then asks for a show of hands for anyone needing healing for any kind of problem — physical, spiritual, mental, financial. He asks the believers to lay hands on these people and there is a general prayer time. A prayer request sheet passed around earlier for you to write the name and the need of "anyone you promise to tell we are praying for in Yeshua's name" is now read aloud and quickly, corporately prayed over. As the people throw their arms around one another and begin to sing, you are especially touched by the love of these people, who pray aloud corporately for the needs of people not even there.

You enjoy the social time and the refreshments afterward, and you are already looking forward to the special event announced for next week. As you prepare to leave, you are given a copy of the Bible and a document called "What Is

Messianic Judaism?" You are asked to read it and to return it so you can be given another document which is its sequel. Attached to the document is an attractive brochure giving the location, phone and educational program and other information about the Messianic Synagogue as well as the time of the Friday night and other services. As the host and hostess give you a warm farewell, you are personally invited to attend Friday night services at the sheul.

In the weeks ahead, the phone ministers, bus ministers, and the mail will keep you in touch with the exciting on-going life of this fully operative Messianic Synagogue. The notes you receive in your various Torah classes are sequentially numbered, so you begin to want to attend regularly in order to compile a complete book of everything that is passed out. In a very warm and joyful way, you are being drawn into a life of commitment and learning and service in a growing Messianic Synagogue that is so wonderfully Jewish you're not ashamed to tell anyone in your family that you go there.

BIBLIOGRAPHY FOR A HOME TORAH STUDY TEACHER

Alexander Whyte, *Bible Characters from the Old Testament and the New Testament*, Zondervan.

Alfred Edersheim, *The Life and Times of Jesus the Messiah*, Eerdmans.

Ben-Yehuda's Pocket English-Hebrew, Hebrew-English Dictionary, Washington Press.

Fred Kogos, *Instant Yiddish*, Citadel Press.

Hebrew/English Old Testament, American Bible Society.

Henry Spalding, *Encyclopedia of Jewish Humor*, Jonathan David Publishers.

Herbert Lockyer, *All the Messianic Prophecies of the Bible*, Zondervan.

J. Oswald Sanders, *A Spiritual Clinic: Problems of Christian Discipleship*, Moody Pocket Books.

Jewish Digest, 257 Mamaroneck Road, Scarsdale, New York, 10583.

Magil's Linear School Bible, The Five Books of Moses, Hebrew Publishing Company.

New Bible Commentary (one volume commentary on the entire Bible), Eerdmans.

R. T. France, *Jesus and the Old Testament*, Tyndale Press.

The New English Bible.

APPENDIX

The New Testament in Hebrew and English, the Society for
Distributing the Holy Scriptures to the Jews, 237 Shaftes-
bury Avenue, London, W.C.2.
Thompson Chain Reference Bible.
Victor Buksbagen, *The Gospel in the Feasts of Israel*, pub-
lished by the Spearhead Press, 1218 Chestnut Street,
Philadelphia, Pennsylvania 19107.

YOUR MESSIANIC FRIDAY NIGHT SERVICE

Since the saving confession is not the Shema (James 2:19),
but that Yeshua is Lord (Romans 10:9), it is important to sing
the total confession of Messianic Judaism. Therefore, when
you come to page 110 in your Friday night liturgy and sing
the Shema, be sure to also sing "Ah-don-nye, Ah-don-nye,
Yeshua Ha Mah-shee-ach Ah-don-nye. Ba-rooch Ah-tah, Ah-
don-nye, Elo-hey-noo, Yeshua Ha Mashiach Ah-don-nye"
(sung to the tune of "He Is Lord"). (If your Hebrew is rusty,
see Exhibit G.)

God will teach your synagogue your own musical settings
of the traditional Friday night prayers, both from your own
experience, from cantorial record albums, and from attending
other synagogues.

Don't neglect the Oneg Shabbat after your Friday night
service. It is during this refreshment-social time that the
chavaroot of Yeshua will be experienced and believers will
have opportunity for informal sharing with unbelievers.

What is true for your home Torah studies is also true for
your sheul: if you have a full calendar of spiritually edifying,
exciting special events, your own people will be your best
publicity agents and will be drawn into more faithful attendance and commitment themselves, even as they bring their
friends and family to your services.

YOUR ACTS 2:42 SUNDAY

Making disciples is drawing lines and persuading men to
cross them. When you ask Jewish people to respond in faith
to Yeshua by getting into the water, standing up to take the
broken matzoh of the Lord's Supper, or coming forward to
receive the membership manual, you are drawing the lines
sharply and unambiguously. The result will be you will be
making disciples. Acts 2:42 Sunday, the last Sunday of the

144

month, will be your opportunity to reap the harvest from each month's home Bible studies as new believers cross the lines of commitment.

A pot luck "Agape Feast" after the service will give each newly baptized believer a further taste of chavaroot from what he has experienced in his first Lord's Supper. Further-more, many only peripherally committed believers will be drawn by the food and will be greatly impressed by the Lord's Supper service, especially if their refusal to obey God in the mikveh has made them ineligible to partake of it. When Jewish people see that responding to the Gospel is a very Jewish thing to do because baptism is a mikveh-bris and the Lord's Supper is a Seder, then the tension is on them to con-fess Yeshua as Lord by getting into the water in order to receive the Lord's Seder. That discipling tension will be applied the last Sunday of every month at your sheul, with proven success. The regular monthly cycle of Acts 2:42 Sundays will force you to keep your outreach machinery well oiled and it will insure larger crowds and regular chavaroot for your people on the Lord's Day.

TRAINING YOUR FISHERMEN

Besides the judicious record-keeping of guest books and mailing lists, you need a dedicated core of Jewish women to minister on the phone and a dedicated core of men to drive cars and buses to pick the people up. Exhibit A in the Appen-dix is a phone minister's presentation which your ladies can use to persuade people to come to your meetings, using the Word of God (Exhibit B) to overcome their excuses as well as to minister to their needs, and to bring them before the Body for prayer. The phone ministers should report the fruit of their labor on the Phone Minister Monthly Report Forms (Exhibit C) to a transportation-and-follow-up coordinator. If your phone ministers can each develop a nucleus of regular bus or car riders, they can add to this core new names sent to them weekly by the coordinator, who has access to the office backlog of guest books and referrals.

Your bus ministers can model the selfless love of Yeshua by their untiring generosity in picking the people up each week as their undershepherd and friend in the Lord. A dedi-cated bus minister is one of the most persuasive proofs of the reality of Yeshua's self-denying love. Anyone who would be so lowly of heart to be the chauffeur of these Jewish people week after week will be among the greatest people in your synagogue (Mark 10:43-45). Many unsaved Jewish people, even those who have automobiles, would never trouble to bring themselves to your home Torah study without a bus minister who cared enough to make sure they got there (Mark 14:38). Only if your bus ministers and your phone ministers and your people in general have a burden for lost souls will your synagogue grow.

Your transportation-and-follow-up coordinator should maintain a large multi-ring master address book with coded alphabetically rearrangeable insert cards. Arranged in tiers, dozens of names and loads of coded information can be viewed at a glance. Thus the coordinator processes all the names through five possible follow-up recommendations: 1) WAIT and have the same phone minister contact the person later, 2) TRANSFER the name to another phone minister, 3) send someone to make a PERSONAL VISIT, 4) send a friendly LETTER of warning to Gospel rejectors, 5) cease communication because the person is ALREADY COMMITTED to another Body of Yeshua. The coordinator must process the recommendations of the Phone Minister Monthly Reports until each name has been recycled through 1), 2) and 3) and either becomes a regular attender or is processed through 4) and 5) (see Exhibit D).

The men and women who do this ministry need regular meetings and retreats to expand their commitment and ability. These are the fishers-of-men that will be the key harvest laborers of Messianic Judaism, and they should be trained and loved as carefully as Yeshua trained and loved the twelve.

The follow-up coordinator should also function as the Binder Document Librarian. The Binder Document Librarian keeps track of each binder document as it leaves its binder, does its Holy Spirit-empowered discipling work, and returns. Because every binder has a code number which appears on each of its respective four documents, it is simple for the Binder Document Librarian to file the returned documents back into their proper binders as they are brought in by the home Torah teachers and the mailman. Furthermore, because the BINDER INDEX FILE has four sectional divisions for Parts I, II, III, and IV, a single 3 x 5 index card can be brought forward through the four sectional divisions as the inquirer moves from part to part, checking out and returning the documents. The Binder Document Librarian has a MASTER BINDER SHEET which tells him which binders are in service and whom they are serving. If Brother A has Binder 43 and the Binder Document Librarian wants to know how he's doing, he can open Brother A's binder to see which document is missing. Then the Binder Document Librarian can go to the appropriate section of the BINDER INDEX FILE, look up Brother A alphabetically, pull his 3 x 5 index card, and check to see if he has had the document checked out to him for a reasonable time. If he has, he should be followed up to return the document so that he can either make a decision to proceed in obedience to the next step or let someone else use what would have become his binder had he decided to become a disciple.

The 3 x 5 card has his name, his binder code number, the numbers of the documents so far issued to him and returned, and the dates he checked them out and returned them as well as the date and name of any follow-up worker assigned to see him and the results. With this information before him, the Binder Document Librarian can coordinate prayer and ministry for the inquirer and can serve the Spirit of God in moving the inquirer toward incorporation as a disciple of Yeshua and a synagogue member.

THE BUS MINISTER:
A POTENTIAL SYNAGOGUE PLANTER

Since the pastoring task involves both feeding and gathering the sheep, a bus minister who is faithful in gathering may in time be entrusted with the task of feeding (Luke 16:10). Therefore, the bus ministers are all potential teachers and synagogue planters, especially since only ten men are required to make a minyon and each home Torah study is a potential house synagogue. Each synagogue, once it is established, should set goals to raise up a core of bus ministers who are home Torah study teacher interns, each preparing to go out and plant a daughter house synagogue in another area. Although these home Torah study teachers will not receive a salary, they will find re-employment, perhaps in their old line of work, wherever the Lord sends them. These men will spend their part-time hours each week, gathering and feeding the sheep, picking people up, bringing them weekly to a Jewish home Torah study, teaching them, giving them the mikveh and the Lord's Seder and helping them celebrate their faith through the traditions of Messianic Judaism, especially in and through the Friday night Erev Shabbat service.

In this way, little house synagogues will spread throughout the world, and each one, as it grows up, will begin to support salaried full-time workers, both at home and all over the earth. These mother synagogues will spawn daughter synagogues (like the Great Mother Synagogue did in Jerusalem 2,000 years ago) as each one raises up an army of bus-ministering, Torah teaching synagogue planters to go out like the 70 (Luke 10:17) wherever the Lord leads. These men and women are the laborers for the end-time harvest of the Jewish people (Romans 11:26). The mother synagogues will keep in contact with their children through the mail and through periodic exchange visits as Messianic Judaism spreads throughout Jewry everywhere.

What are the characteristics of these Jewish fishers-of-men?
1) They are humble and tireless. If a man is too proud or lazy to pick up sheep he will find himself feeding an empty Jewish living room.
2) They must be committed to the Word of God. If a man is half-hearted in his commitment to the Scriptures, so will be the quality of, and the response to, his teaching.
3) They must be committed to sustaining Jewish traditions. The Jewish synagogues they plant must remain Jewish, generation after generation, until the Lord comes. This means these men must be zealous to maintain their Jewish heritage, and to celebrate their Messianic, Scriptural faith in and through that precious heritage and all of its customs and observances. They must establish these traditions and not abandon them to suit the whims of any non-Jewish believers who may come along. However, these latter need not be feared as corrosive elements that will in time transform the Jewish culture synagogues into Gentile culture synagogues. Rather, their minority presence may serve as the watchword to preclude Messianic synagogues with healthy Jewish cultural orientation from becoming exclusivistic post-Pauline abominations.

4) They must keep the issue clear. The crucial issue between Messianic Judaism and any other sort of Judaism centers on the hope of the resurrection from the dead. The only question is whether there is such a hope and whether that hope has been realized in the historical resurrection of Yeshua Ha Mashiach. Is Yeshua the King of Israel or not? Is he alive today to rule the hearts of men even as, in the Age to Come, he will rule the world — or not? There is no other issue.

A PERSONAL NOTE

I attended a Jewish home Bible study in California 2½ years ago. I looked at the Jewish faces in the room and saw how much Yeshua meant to our people. To see Jewish people at last discovering their Messiah so touched me that I began to pray for them, that God would reach more and more. At that time I was an actor and had been making some television commercials.

One Tuesday morning at 10:00 o'clock I told the Lord Yeshua that if he would give me a national television commercial, then I would buy a mini-bus to take more of our people to that home Bible study. The next day the telephone rang. It was my agent. I had been cast in a national television commercial! Without even auditioning! Shocked beyond belief, I went to work the same day. When I asked the casting director why he decided to choose me, he said, "Your face came to my mind and I knew I had to use you for the part. I found you in the Players Directory." I asked, "When did you decide to use me?" and the man said, "Tuesday morning around 10:00 o'clock." That was the exact time I had prayed.

Besides a bus and a Bible, God gave me a Jewish home, this book and a phone minister. By following up each Jewish inquirer on the phone and in person, I saw a Messianic synagogue planted practically overnight.

Had I never driven a bus or my car to faithfully pick up people each week, I would never have taught a Torah study; had I never taught a Torah study, I would never have planted a Messianic synagogue; had I never planted a Messianic synagogue, I would never have written this book (Luke 16:10; John 21:15-17).

APPENDIX

It is the prayer of Ray Gannon and I that your sheul will have many bus ministers who will be faithful in gathering the lost sheep of Israel in order that they may be entrusted to feed them and go out from your midst to shepherd flocks all over the world.

October, 1974
Phil Goble
Encino, California

SAMPLE PHONE MINISTER PRESENTATION

"Hello, is this Mrs. _____? I'm Mrs. _____
from _____ Messianic Synagogue, and I'd like to invite you to
our ____(day)____ evening Torah study. We meet at the lovely
home of Mr. and Mrs. _____ in _____, and we
have an unusually warm time of study and interchange and
refreshments together . . . doesn't that sound appealing to you?

We can pick you up in our mini-bus, of course, and bring
you home. Could you be ready between 6:30 and 7:00 p.m.?
(Ignore excuses at this point.)

Mrs. _____, I want to give you my telephone number
. . . do you have a pencil? It's ____(give your phone number)____.
Now, could you please give me your street address? Is that a
house or an apartment? (Ask for the apartment number.)
Mrs. _____, could you give me your nearest cross street?
(Now, you're ready to prayerfully and emphatically deal with
excuses.)

Mrs. _____, is there any reason you couldn't come
this week? (Check your Scripture sheet to begin dealing with
her excuses.) I see, I know what you mean. But Mrs. _____,
remember what the Word of God says . . . (Read or quote
the Scripture appropriate to her excuse.)

(At this point, she will probably pull out another excuse.
Be ready for it with your Scripture sheet.) I understand,
Mrs. _____, and I appreciate what you're saying.
Still, though, the Word of God says . . . (Quote the Scripture
appropriate to her second excuse.)

(Is she still excuse-hunting?) Then say, Mrs. _____, if
this week is bad for you, let's set it up for the following week.

(Is she still excuse-hunting?) Mrs. _____, tell me
frankly . . . how much probability is there that you could
come if I should call you later? I see. One final question,
Mrs. _____, and this is very important. Do you have
any needs that you would appreciate prayers for? (help her:)
Financial? Physical? Depression? Spiritual? (When she tells
you her need, say this:) Well, Mrs. _____, I just want
to quickly share with you what the Word of God says about
your need. (Read the appropriate Scripture.) Now, Mrs.
_____, I want you to have my word on one thing.
_____ evening at our Torah study, there's going to be a house
full of Jewish people praying for your need in Yeshua's name,
so expect a miracle, okay? I'll be talking with you. Goodbye."

POCKET HOOKS FOR PRAYING FISHERMEN
(MEMORIZE OR READ)

"IS THERE ANY REASON WHY YOU COULDN'T COME?"
A. *Too busy?* "You are anxious and troubled about many things; but one thing is necessary: choose what cannot be taken away from you" (Luke 10:41-42). "Cast all your cares upon him because he cares about you" (I Peter 5:7).
B. *Afraid of converting?* "We are the true Jews who worship God in the Spirit, whose pride is in Yeshua Ha Mashiach, and who put no confidence in mere externals" (Philippians 3:3).
C. *Too much to give up?* "But what shall it profit a man, if he shall gain the whole world and lose his own soul?" (Mark 8:36).
D. *I have my own ideas.* But the Lord says, "I will give them one heart and one way that they may fear me forever" (Jeremiah 32:39). "All we like sheep have gone astray: we have turned everyone to his own way; and the Lord hath laid on him the iniquity of us all" (Isaiah 53:6).
E. *Not now—maybe later?* "Boast not thyself of tomorrow; for thou knowest not what a day may bring forth" (Proverbs 27:1).
F. *Involved in a cult?* "If anyone teaches a gospel at variance with the gospel we preached to you, let him be accursed" (Galatians 1:8). "Let no one be found among you who practices divination, or a fortune teller, or an augur, or a sorcerer, or a charmer, or a medium, or a witch, or a necromancer. For whoever does these things is an abomination to the Lord" (Deuteronomy 18:10-12).
G. *Back-slidden baptized believer?* "Do not stay away from our meetings, as some do, but rather come encourage one another; for if we willfully persist in disobedience after receiving the knowledge of the truth, no sacrifice remains: only a fearful prospect of judgment and a fierce fire which will consume God's enemies" (Hebrews 10:25-27).
H. *Yeshua was just a man?* "Unto us a child is born and his name shall be called Almighty God" (in Hebrew 'el gabor') (Isaiah 9:6). "And now Father, glorify me in thy own presence with the glory which I had with thee before the world began" (John 17:5).
I. *Won't explain?* "Shall not God search this out? For he knows the secrets of the heart" (Psalm 44:21).

(Continued on next page.)

152

"DO YOU HAVE ANY NEEDS THAT YOU WOULD APPRECIATE OUR PRAYERS FOR?"

P. *Illness?* If you will diligently listen to the voice of the Lord thy God, and will do that which is right in his sight and will give ear to his commandments and keep all his statutes, I will put none of these diseases upon thee, which I have brought upon the Egyptians: for I am the Lord that healeth thee" (Exodus 15:26).

Q. *Depression?* Mental suffering can help us grow in obedience. The Scripture says, "Even Yeshua learned to obey through what he suffered and so qualified to become a source of unending salvation to those who obey him" (Hebrews 5:8-9).

R. *Financial?* "And my God will supply all your wants out of the magnificence of his riches in Yeshua Ha Mashiach (Philippians 4:19). "Set your mind on God's kingdom and his justice before everything else, and all the rest will come to you as well" (Matthew 6:33).

S. *Spiritually oppressed?* "Resist the enemy in the name of Yeshua and he will flee from you" (James 4:7).

T. *New believer needing spiritual nurture?* "And those who accepted the Gospel took the mikveh-bris of water immersion and they met persistently to hear the apostolic preaching, to have fellowship, to celebrate the Lord's Seder and to pray" (Acts 2:41-42).

PHONE MINISTER'S MONTHLY REPORT FORM

Phone Minister's Name_____ Month and Year____

1. Is there any reason why you couldn't come this week?
A. Too busy
B. Afraid of converting
C. Too much to give up
D. I have my own ideas
E. Not now . . . maybe later
F. Involved in a cult
G. Back-slidden baptized believer
H. Yeshua was just a man
I. Won't explain
J. Other (write on back)

2. How much probability is there you could come if I should call you later?
K. Don't call me again ever!
L. Don't call us — we'll call you.
M. You can call again, but I probably will not be able to come
N. I'll come later once in a while
O. Other (write on back)

3. Do you have any needs you would appreciate prayers for?
P. Illness
Q. Depression
R. Financial
S. Spiritual
T. New believer needing nurture
U. Other (write on back)

Recommendation
V. Wait before contacting
W. Transfer this name to __
X. Have someone make a personal visit (recommend who on back)
Y. Send friendly warning letter (put address on back)
Z. Already committed to another Body of believers

Note: If the person is not home or is unreachable by phone, write absolutely nothing here but instead make your own notes on the back of this page. Remember, too, if Yeshua needed a quiet time before he ministered, how much more do you! Before you send this to the outreach coordinator on Acts 2:42 Sunday (the last Sunday of the month), save a carbon copy for your own records.

Name	Phone	Day/Time Called	#1	#2	#3	Recommendation
1. ___	___	__/__	___	___	___	___
2. ___	___	__/__	___	___	___	___
3. ___	___	__/__	___	___	___	___
4. ___	___	__/__	___	___	___	___
5. ___	___	__/__	___	___	___	___
6. ___	___	__/__	___	___	___	___

(On a larger page there will be reporting room for more names.)

154

FOLLOW-UP COORDINATOR'S OVERVIEW

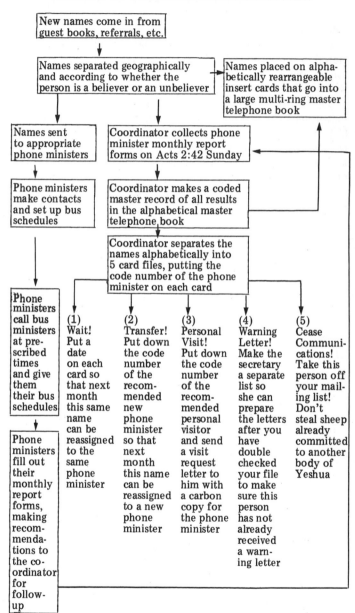

New names come in from guest books, referrals, etc.

Names separated geographically and according to whether the person is a believer or an unbeliever

Names placed on alphabetically rearrangeable insert cards that go into a large multi-ring master telephone book

Names sent to appropriate phone ministers

Coordinator collects phone minister monthly report forms on Acts 2:42 Sunday

Phone ministers make contacts and set up bus schedules

Coordinator makes a coded master record of all results in the alphabetical master telephone book

Coordinator separates the names alphabetically into 5 card files, putting the code number of the phone minister on each card

Phone ministers call bus ministers at pre-scribed times and give them their bus schedules

Phone ministers fill out their monthly report forms, making recommenda-tions to the co-ordinator for follow-up

(1) Wait! Put a date on each card so that next month this same name can be reassigned to the same phone minister

(2) Transfer! Put down the code number of the recom-mended new phone minister so that next month this name can be reassigned to a new phone minister

(3) Personal Visit! Put down the code number of the recom-mended personal visitor and send a visit request letter to him with a carbon copy for the phone minister

(4) Warning Letter! Make the secretary a separate list so she can prepare the letters after you have double checked your file to make sure this person has not already received a warn-ing letter

(5) Cease Communi-cations! Take this person off your mail-ing list! Don't steal sheep already committed to another body of Yeshua

SAMPLE WELCOME LETTER

Dear _____,

Baruch ha shem! We of our Messianic Synagogue so appreciated your attendance that we thought we would let you know. We hope you enjoyed being part of us and that you will consider yourself welcome from now on.

The purpose of our Messianic Synagogue is to be God's instrument for healing and peace in both the Jewish and the Gentile communities. It is also our God-given task to share the Scriptural truths of Messianic Judaism with all people and to raise up our children according to the traditions of our people.

Please consider us your friends and let us see you again soon.

God bless you,

SAMPLE FRIENDLY LETTER OF WARNING
TO GOSPEL REJECTORS

Dear _____,

Our synagogue is a Jewish congregation of believers in the Tenach. Besides our week-end synagogue services, we also meet locally in Jewish homes for Torah study and for chavaroot, and we would enjoy YOU being with us!

We wish that we could tell you all the wonderful blessings that the God of Abraham, Isaac and Jacob has showered on us: the physical healings, the answers to prayer, the love, the joy he has given to us all. Some, who first came to our Jewish home Torah study, skeptical of our motives, are now the happiest and most ardent friends we have.

They too have come to believe the marvelous Good News about the God of Israel — that he sent his own eternal, life-giving Word among us as a Man so that if YOU believe his Word YOU will not perish but have wholesome, abundant life. In the light of this offer of love, God says that there can be no indifference. The Jewish Messiah Yeshua (Jesus' Hebrew name), who is the Divine Word of God In-Person, declares, "He that is not with me is against me." To make no decision to trust and obey the Jewish Messiah Yeshua is in reality a rejection of him. If you choose to reject such love, the God of Israel will honor your choice forever, to your eternal shame and regret. We are far too concerned about you to see you do that!

The Scriptures teach that although many of the Jewish people believed in Yeshua, some refused to obey him because they feared their own people and because they valued their reputation with men more than they valued the honor that comes from God. However, Yeshua declares: "If you love me, you will obey my commands!" Yeshua loved you enough to die for you. But do YOU love Yeshua? He will judge your love on the basis of your obedience to his commands. If you refuse to obey him, he will refuse to believe that you love him. One of Yeshua's commandments to us is that we not stay away from believers' meetings. Please don't disobey him. Transportation to our get-togethers is available to you (call _____). The very wonderful Jewish people of our synagogue care about you and have provided a free Bible for you upon request.

Please accept this letter in the same spirit of love and concern with which it is sent to you. Our purpose is to serve YOU! Please let us know how we can help you.

Your friends,

HEBREW PRONUNCIATION KEY

If your rusty Hebrew keeps you from participating as fully as you would like in the Lord's Seder and the Friday night service, look what you can do. Using this pronunciation key as a teacher, simply study the transliteration for the Lord's Seder and the Friday night service, comparing the transliteration syllable by syllable to the Hebrew. By frequent reference to this pronunciation key, you'll soon be sight reading Hebrew without any crutches whatsoever!

א	silent	ל	L	ת	T
בּ	B	מ	M	ת	T
ב	V	ם	M		AH
ג	G	נ	N		AH
ד	D	ן	N		EH
ה	H	ס	S		EH
ו	V	ע	Silent		OO
ז	Z	פּ	P		EE
ח	CH (gutteral)	פ	F	Left of consonant	OY
ט	T	ף	F		OH
י	Y	צ	TS		OO
כּ	K	ץ	TS	Over the consonant	OH
כ	CH (gutteral)	ק	K		EYE
ך	CH (gutteral) (FINAL)	ר	R		OY
		שׁ	SH		
		שׂ	S		

158

NOTE: To preserve your documents from wear and tear, paperclip them together and cover them in plastic bags. Then issue them in return mailing envelopes and stamp your mailing address on each document. This will help to insure that the documents will be returned to you in good condition for future re-use.